A ROLL OF THE DICE

a story of loss, love
and genetics

Mona Dash

Published by Linen Press, London 2019
8 Maltings Lodge
Corney Reach Way
London
W4 2TT

www.linen-press.com

Cover image: Arcangel
Typeset by Zebedee Design.
Printed and bound by Lightning Source
ISBN 978-1-9996046-3-9

ABOUT THE AUTHOR

Photo by Kashif Haque

Mona Dash is the author of *Untamed Heart* (Tara India Research Press, 2016), *Dawn-Drops* (Writer's Workshop India, 2001) and *A Certain Way* (Skylark Publications UK, 2017). She has a Masters (with distinction) in Creative Writing. Her work has been widely published and awarded. Her short story collection *Let us look Elsewhere* was shortlisted for the 2018 SI Leeds Literary prize for unpublished work. She is a member of The Whole Kahani, a British South Asian Writers collective with two published anthologies.

Mona is a Telecoms Engineer with an MBA and works full time for a global technology organisation. Originally from India, she lives in London.

www.monadash.net
@dash2mona

PRAISE FOR A ROLL OF THE DICE

A profoundly moving and uplifting book about the triumphant survival of life against all odds. It'll go straight into your heart and expand its capacity for feeling. Read it and be changed.

– Neel Mukherjee

Powerful, moving, beautifully observed and wonderfully sensitive. It mines the depths and heights of human love and suffering and is perceptive about family dynamics, the weight of trauma and comfort of family support. The steady accretion of detail and emotion are exceptionally skilful; the book creeps up on you and steals your heart. I couldn't stop reading once I started. I particularly like the observations of daily life in cities – the textured evocation of having to walk and talk, live, love and work in the 'ordinary' world – while going through operatic swings of emotion at the same time. Mona Dash is a powerful, important and fearlessly honest new voice – capable of looking the deepest suffering and the greatest joy full in the face.

– Bidisha

A writer of rare bravery, putting forward a manifesto against the tropes and delighting in subverting expectations.

– Roopa Farooki

A deeply affecting book, touching and beautifully rendered. A powerful read from an exciting new voice.

– Irenosen Okojie

The violets in the mountains have broken the rocks.
    – Tennessee Williams, Camino Real

The violet's message was, 'Keep up the courage, stay true to what you believe in.'
    – Jessica Stern, Denial, A Memoir of Terror

This can only be for you: Kaustubh, ➤Akshyat➤
and very specially Krish.

CONTENTS

INTRODUCTION BY PROFESSOR BOBBY GASPAR

As a junior doctor starting at Great Ormond Street Hospital for Children in London in August 1992, I still remember my first ward round, walking with the medical team from patient to patient. In those old, slightly shabby cubicles, lay the sickest, most vulnerable children I had ever seen in my still-young medical career. I saw small, malnourished infants and children ravaged by infection or suffering the side effects of the treatments that they were going through. I saw babies whose condition had warranted a mere paragraph in my medical textbooks but whose underlying disease was so severe and profound that there were very few treatments available, and for many of whom an early death was almost inevitable. This was my first introduction to SCID (Severe Combined Immuno Deficiency) and the impact of those first encounters were to shape my professional career and have also, to a large extent, shaped my personal life.

So what is SCID? How does it come about and how can we treat it? SCID is extremely rare, so rare that of the 800,000 babies born in the UK per year, only 15-20 will be born with the disease. I will write later about how it may be more common in other parts of the world. The condition affects the immune system and our ability to protect ourselves from the myriad bacteria, viruses and fungi that inhabit our everyday lives. For those of us with normal immune systems, we have specialised white cells in our blood stream that can fight these infections and even though we may get occasional coughs, cold and other problems, we usually get through them. Now imagine a child with SCID who is born with none of these cells, or whose cells do not work properly. These babies are usually born normally to unsuspecting parents who have no idea of what is to come. In the first few months, protected by their mother's antibodies that were passed on in the womb or by breast feeding, they can grow and develop normally. But after three or four months, when their own immune system has to kick in and protect them, they start to develop problems. Very often this is a cough or cold or diarrhoea, looking at first like the common problems that normal babies have, so family physicians and general practitioners respond with either reassurance that it will get better with time or with a course of antibiotics. Except of course, with no immune system to fight the infection, the problem doesn't get better. Then, for parents of SCID babies, a familiar odyssey begins. Parents, watching their child not improving and even getting worse, take the child back and forth to the family doctor or sometimes resort to the emergency room at their local hospital. Unless the doctors are very quick on the uptake, they still think the problem will resolve itself because most doctors have never seen a case of SCID and most never will. And so the condition worsens and finally the baby ends up being admitted to hospital for more expert care and treatment.

At this stage, a number of things can happen. It is essential that a severe problem with the immune system is recognised very quickly. A few simple tests to look at the immune system can offer a fast diagnosis of SCID which can then lead to a more intensive treatment regime and referral to a specialist centre such as Great Ormond Street where experts in the disease can decide on the right treatment options. All too sadly, for some children, it may be too late and their first severe infection may also be their last. They will die at their local hospital or when they arrive at the specialist centre because the infections and the complications are too far advanced.

It is important to remember that SCID was only reported as a disease in 1968 and prior to that, all babies with SCID would die in the first year or two of life without a diagnosis. The vulnerability to infection and the bacteria in the outside world means that special precautions had to be taken to prevent them from coming into contact with infections so they needed to be cared for in special cubicles with limited contact with their family, even siblings. In some cases, babies were nursed in specially designed plastic bubbles to protect them from infections and so the term 'Bubble babies' was coined and has captured the popular imagination. In the most extreme and well known case, David Vetter, a boy with SCID, was nursed in a special bubble until the age of 12, after which he had a bone marrow transplant (more of which later) and died.

Even with current treatments, the severity of an infection and the complexity of the treatments mean that a number of children still die. The figures for the outcome of SCID are variable, but in some reports, of all babies born with SCID, up to 60% may die, some before they get to curative treatment and some even after treatment.

SCID also comes in a number of different flavours. The problem is due to a mistake in a single gene which means that the cells of the bone marrow, which are the factory cells from which our white cells and immune system develop, do not have the correct signals to work properly and can't grow functioning white cells. There are about eighteen different genes that, if affected, can cause SCID. In one of them, the gene lies on the X chromosome which means that women can carry the disease and their male children may be affected. This was the case for Mona's son, Krish, and why both boys in his family were affected. In other cases, the gene is carried by both parents and can affect 1 in 4 boys or girls in the family. In parts of the world where there is more marriage within extended families and so more family members carrying the defective gene, more babies may be born with SCID. There are no definitive figures but in parts of the Middle East, it is estimated that approximately 1:5,000-1:10,000 babies may be affected whereas in Europe or the USA, the figure is likely to be1:50,000 or more. Of course, in poor countries where there are fewer resources, less specialist care and fewer diagnostic opportunities, babies with SCID will die early of infection. There will be no diagnosis because in such areas, babies dying from infection at an early age is not so unusual. As a result, we don't really know the burden of SCID in many parts of the world.

As for treatment, this is still very limited. The first important thing is to identify the disease, start treating infections quickly and prevent further infections by using antibiotics and antibodies. However, these are just holding measures and what a SCID baby really needs is a new immune system with properly functioning white cells. Until recently, the only way to do this was through a bone marrow transplant which still remains the standard treatment. Essentially, this involves taking bone marrow cells from a healthy individual or donor and giving that to the SCID baby so they can grow a new immune system. But this in itself can cause a number of dilemmas and problems. The best donor is a brother or sister who is a full 'match'[1] but not every child has one. Then we have to look for somebody unrelated who is a 'match' which can take some time. We can also use a parent who, of course, is readily available and is willing to donate to save their child's life, but parents are usually only half matches for their own children. We also have to consider whether to treat the child with chemotherapy to make space in the marrow for the incoming donor cells. In the case of SCID, some transplants can be done without chemotherapy, but you risk the possibility that it may not work or may only partially restore the immune system. Or you give chemotherapy to ensure a better chance of the treatment working but this now carries the risks of the chemotherapy itself which can be damaging to various organs, especially in babies with severe infection or in very young babies. So, although treatment options are available, each one carries benefits and risks, and this is what we discuss amongst ourselves as the medical and nursing team, and with each family before a decision about treatment is made. Over the years, the chances of success with transplants have got better for a variety of reasons, but we still can't guarentee that if a child comes into transplant with a severe infection, the procedure will be successful.

---

1 The best donor is one where there is a matching between certain markers on the surface of white cells between the recipient (the SCID baby) and the donor. We usually look for 10 markers and so a 10/10 match is ideal. Parents are often only half matches, 5/10 or 6/10, and this can cause problems because some donor cells see the child as different and can attack the child's organs. If we want to use a mismatched parent as a donor, we have to remove those specific donor cells.

More recently, there have been developments that can improve the outcome for babies with SCID. One area is gene therapy and this has been the focus of my research work for the past twenty years. We know that SCID happens because an important gene in the immune system is missing or not working and so if we can put a working copy of the gene into the child's own bone marrow cells, then those cells will have the right gene and give the correct signals to grow a new immune system. And using the child's own cells has many advantages: they cannot be rejected and they do not fight the child's own body. We have now used this approach for two different genetic forms of SCID and have shown it to be very successful. Currently, the treatment is only available in very few specialised centres in Europe and in the UK, but there are moves to make it more widely available.

Probably, the biggest impact on the outcome of SCID is new born screening. We know that the best results from a transplant are when a baby goes into the procedure without having had any previous severe infections. We can do this when there is already a family history of SCID and so, the baby is diagnosed at birth and can be protected straightaway with prophylactic antibiotics and antibodies and an early transplant performed. In such cases the survival after transplant can be 90% or more. In 2005, a test was developed whereby a small sample of blood could be taken from babies at birth and checked to see if they had SCID. The development of this technique has had major consequences especially in the US. At the time of writing, following a huge amount of lobbying and patient advocacy, every state in the US is now screening all newborn babies for SCID. This has been an extremely successful programme with very few babies with SCID being missed and the overall survival for SCID now reaching 90%. In other parts of the world, progress has been slower but there is now national screening in Israel, Norway, New Zealand and numerous pilot programmes in Europe. I have felt very strongly that a similar programme should be implemented in the UK and have campaigned for UK SCID newborn screening since 2011. I have received support from many parents of children with SCID including Mona Dash who understands first hand why this would make a huge, significant difference. In 2017, the UK Department of Health agreed to undertake a pilot scheme to evaluate SCID screening which, once their concerns are addressed and satisfied, would lead to a national programme.

I've written a lot here about SCID the disease and its treatment, but I would like to focus too on the impact it has on families as well as how it has shaped me as a physician looking after affected children. The suffering families go through with a SCID baby is immense. Unlike some other genetic diseases which may be manifest at birth, with SCID there is nothing that tells the parent there is anything wrong. So when, after a few months, the infections start and no doctor can give an explanation or diagnosis, this unexplained deterioration of a child's health comes as a complete shock to the parents. It is also a condition that remains with the child, the parents and the family for a very long time. From initial problems, through diagnosis, through treatment, bone marrow transplant, potential complications, the whole process may take many months and often years. Through that time, the emotional burden is enormous; the distress of seeing a child suffering and getting worse with no diagnosis, the agony of visits to intensive care, watching your baby paralysed and ventilated, the shock of finding that your child has a life threatening condition and the rollercoaster that accompanies a bone marrow transplant where small improvements can be followed by major complications.

Having watched many families go through this, I am always amazed. I am amazed at their strength, their courage, their dignity and in the end the sheer fight they show for their baby. And I always ask myself, how would I cope in their position, if my own baby had SCID? Would I find the strength to be there every day, selflessly, at the bedside, watching time pass, wondering whether my child will survive, whether a donor will be found, whether they will survive chemotherapy? But, I suppose, you have to because there is no other choice. As a parent, you have to fight for your child's life. Understanding that, and putting yourself in the parents' shoes, means you can and have to accept many things when you start that doctor/parent relationship. If I was the parent, I would want to explore every treatment option. I would want to question where the evidence is for the treatment you – the doctor – is proposing. I would want to question why you are doing one thing when other experts are doing something else. I would want to know if it will work, how it will work, when it will work....and in the end no question is too small and every question should be answered as best as you can.

And this was my relationship with Mona. She fought and she fought for her child. She needed to know everything so that she could offer him the best chance of survival. She stood between him and death and she knew that it was her responsibility, her mother's will that was necessary to give him that chance of life. And she asked question after question until she was sure that Krish was going to get the best treatment possible and have the best chance of life.

Over the years, I have realised that our role as physicians in caring for these children is an extraordinary privilege because we are part of the most important decisions that a family will ever make - decisions about the life of their child. And with that privilege, comes enormous responsibility and duty to provide the best care possible and to offer the parents your knowledge and expertise in as fair, unbiased and as transparent a manner as possible. It can mean sometimes having to give information that they may find hard to accept. It also means explaining concepts and choices in a way that is accessible. And I can say with absolute certainty, that this relationship with the families and children, and being part of their illness and their treatment, is the most satisfying and rewarding role that I have experienced in my long career.

Professor Bobby Gaspar
Professor of Paediatrics and Immunology
UCL Great Ormond Street Institute of Child Health

SECTION 1 – RUPTURE – FEAR

1

I could feel the fever climbing.

It was a Thursday, in October, in 2006, in my home in London. Nothing unusual about the day. I was exactly fourteen weeks and five days pregnant. I was working from home and planned to attend my body balance class in the evening. Inspired by the perfectly toned pregnant women who dexterously managed dancer and warrior poses, I was looking forward to completing the rest of my pregnancy in yogic perfection.

But by early evening, I was feeling feverish. While I normally wouldn't care about a mild temperature, I knew I couldn't, shouldn't, take a risk. Giving up the vision of doing graceful Tai Chi moves with my baby bump, I settled on the sofa. I consoled myself that I could go the following week. As always my laptop was with me; a couple more emails to complete and then I would get something to eat and have an early night.

I could still feel the fever climbing.

The first trimester had been a worrying time for us because there had been some mild bleeding or 'spotting' from as early as six weeks. Several times I had been sent to the early scan unit in the local hospital but as the weeks passed, the episodes lessened, and at the milestone of fourteen weeks and five days, that Thursday, I was finally beginning to relax. I would breeze through the second trimester, supposedly a more peaceful, restful time.

I should explain what the early scan unit is. It sat not within but on the periphery of the maternity ward. Here they placed a little device on your stomach and checked the heartbeat, checked *if* there was a heartbeat, and either assured you of the viability of the pregnancy or advised you to give up on this one and try again. They gave you a picture of the scan, grey circles on black paper, and pointed at the bean shape embedded in the centre. They said, 'Look, that's the embryo, that's your baby!' or 'Sorry, dear, but you can treasure this as a keepsake.' There was a sense of desperation in the little waiting room and a dividing line between those who would lose their babies too early and those who would bear their children and their dreams. Cards and messages from parents covered the walls.

Every time I was scanned and heard the loud duk-duk-duk-duk inside me, a wide smile would flash on the nurse's face. 'Baby's fine!' I imagined writing a happy, flowery card to this kind, maternal-looking nurse in my second trimester.

I worked as a solution sales manager with travelling an integral, almost the main aspect of the job. Some days ago, I had taken a train and gone into the depths of High Wycombe for a meeting and in a coffee break had gone to the toilet only to find more of those dreaded little red spots. I could hardly concentrate for the rest of the meeting. The next day I was back in the early scan unit and thankfully the nurse said, 'Baby's fine.' But I had to stop travelling until I reached the next milestone at the start of the second trimester when everything was meant to stabilise. So I had to tell my boss that I needed time off.

Mr. Smith, my gynaecologist, had established me on a daily dose of Clexane injections. One of his previous blood tests had shown a high factor of protein C. I didn't quite know what that meant nor why I had developed it but these subcutaneous injections, given just under the skin, were necessary because otherwise I might be prone to miscarriage.

So I'd learnt to inject myself in the stomach every day. Keep your hand steady, place the needle against the skin of your stomach, pierce carefully at an angle making sure you are not puncturing a blood vessel. It's easy, don't worry, I told myself. After feeling the sharp prick, I carefully put away the used needle in the waste bin provided by the local surgery. The injections were to continue all through the pregnancy, a part of my routine – eat, brush teeth, inject, read, sleep. The bin stood next to my bed and filled up with sharps, like a time counter.

In a week, I was to have a special early gender scan in King's College, London. The result – boy or girl – was crucial. Not just in one of those pink or blue nursery ways, not in an Asian 'I must have a boy' way, but in a far more crucial-to-life-itself way.

Because I could never forget what had happened before, six years earlier.

It was in the kitchen, that Thursday of the mounting fever, after I'd placed my plate in the sink, that it happened. A quick moment. No warning, no pain, no noise and suddenly a thick pool of colourless liquid at my feet. 'Amniotic fluid', I heard myself mumble. Even though I'd never seen it, I just knew. I stared at the gel-like liquid for a while, thick and unspreading on the floor and knew it was the fluid inside the uterus, the fluid that surrounds and protects the baby, essential to its development. Fragments from school Biology lessons flashed through my mind. I can't remember now, was it my hand which reached for some kitchen towels and mopped up the liquid? Or did I rush to the

24

bathroom first and then come back to clean the floor? Did I stare for seconds or minutes, looking at something from deep inside me out there in the open, something that until a moment ago was next to my baby? I don't remember exactly what I did, but soon, trying to stay calm, I went back to my sofa and called my husband. He was out for dinner with some colleagues.

'Hello? Err, hello, there was this thing now…you know… fluid…,' I blurted.

'More bleeding?' He was in the heart of some London pub, loud voices around him, but I heard the worry in his voice.

'No blood, no, not even a speck. It's liquid…I mean, fluid,' I said. If it had been a bright pool of blood on the cream tiled floor, I would have panicked. A colourless pool of liquid, though unusual, looked harmless.

'Fluid? Oh, then that's not too bad. I'll be home soon. We will call the midwife in the morning. She'll know what to do.'

He sounded composed so maybe it was all right. I should rest now. I should go upstairs and get into bed. That's all I needed to do. Just sleep and let the fever ease. Instead, I reached for my laptop and searched 'loss of fluid in second trimester.' A few links came up – low water, loss of amniotic fluid, leaking water, but it was the third or fourth link on the list that caught my eye. An unknown term – PPROM (Pre-term Premature Rupture of Membranes). The word itself sounded violent.

What I read was terrifying. A premature rupture of membranes referred to a loss of amniotic fluid before thirty-seven weeks. The amniotic fluid is crucial and fulfils several functions; it helps protect and cushion the baby inside the sac and protects both the baby and the uterus against infection. It also plays a vital role in the development of internal organs like the lungs and kidneys. The prognosis was grim. 90% of women who suffered a preterm rupture went on to experience labour within forty-eight hours. Even if the pregnancy continued, there was a high risk of prematurity and a higher risk of death due to pulmonary hypoplasia – undeveloped lungs – at birth. The baby would die like a fish out of water. Unexplained, rare, no treatment, death, premature labour, infection, termination, death, death, death – the same words recurred in article after article.

But this couldn't be my diagnosis! I was only fourteen weeks into the pregnancy. Surely there was time for the sac to patch itself and heal? Besides, after all that had happened to me the first time around, and with my concerns about what could still happen after the birth, the pregnancy was the one thing I had assumed would be problem free.

I didn't call my husband again as I knew he would tell me not to self-diagnose. His take on the internet was that while it was a source of information, equally you could diagnose yourself with cancer after a mild rash. In fact, I didn't think of calling anyone, and eventually, laptop shut down, I went upstairs. I tried to sleep but some of the stories played on in my mind. Some women had stressful pregnancies and premature deliveries, but healthy children now. There were many whose babies died the minute they were born, their lungs too rigid to breathe. Death didn't sit well on babies. I knew. I had seen it with my own eyes. I dug deeper into the duvet, shivering with the fever and fear.

I was woken by a cold sensation. My husband was standing in the darkness, holding a strip of wet cloth on my forehead.

'What are you doing?'

'You're burning with fever. I thought this would help.'

It all came back. The mosaic of nightmares closed on me. The fluid. I told him about, the stories I'd read.

'But there has been no more leaking after that, isn't it?' he asked.

I didn't know what to say. The shock of that moment – the realisation of what shouldn't happen but had happened – numbed me.

I went to the toilet and checked. There didn't seem to be any further leaking so maybe everything was fine now. We had to wait the night out and would call the midwife, Claire, and Dr. Patel, our GP, in the morning. They would find a way. Neither of us thought of going to A&E. When I had my first episode of spotting about six weeks into the pregnancy, we'd rushed to emergency and waited for hours to be seen. Going there now, in the middle of the night, when I wasn't in pain or bleeding, didn't seem necessary. Besides, in A&E we would be seen by a doctor with no background knowledge of my case. And I needed my fantastic gynaecologist, Mr. Smith. I needed someone who knew and understood what to do especially for me, specifically for me, because of everything that had happened before.

I tried to go back to sleep, hazy, praying. God, please help, please help. The night had to end. Tomorrow there would be a solution.

But memories came rushing back. I was back on that fateful day when my life changed irrevocably. I was back in that scene which was always on Play, that scene which part of me never stopped re-enacting, wherever I was or whatever I was doing. That scene, that day, from years ago, from the city I had never returned to, from the country I had left, ran on a never-ending reel. The date was 22nd June, 2000.

22nd June 2000, Calcutta, India

A terrified heart, dark brown sandals rushing up the stairs to Flat 6 on the third floor. The door is open. People are waiting in silence.

The footsteps are mine, the living room is mine, and the people inside are waiting for me – the mother. Of course the mother is expected to be present in a situation like this. The centre of attention. A huge responsibility to behave in a manner befitting the tragedy.

'Please come back, as soon as you can. Both of you.' My mother-in-law's call had come just minutes after I'd reached my office that morning. I knew that unless things were bad, she wouldn't call us back from work. I didn't dare ask and face the truth.

'Sorry, guys, I need to leave. Looks like my baby's very unwell.' I spoke calmly to my colleagues. My husband had already left his office and was on his way to pick me up. They nodded briefly, not realising how unwell was unwell.

It was only ten o'clock but the June heat had settled into the morning. I looked out at the familiar crowded roads as we drove back. Neither of us said a word. My heart felt as it was being squeezed tight. Roughly. I felt it physically contracting.

Yet as I ran up those stairs into stillness, into that waiting void, I was still hoping my heart had been lying. I was still hoping that life hadn't deserted us. A dread, a ghoulish curiosity gripped me.

A slow murmur rises from the room as I enter. 'The mother,' someone whispers. I don't return anyone's glance. The door to my bedroom is directly opposite the entrance. I push it open.

He is lying on the bed. Quiet. Still. The air-conditioner whirrs. The room is cool. My baby is wearing a thin white t-shirt and blue shorts with Coca Cola written in black. Ordinary clothes until he is given a bath and changed into a smarter outfit. His face is calm. His curls blow gently in the breeze from the fan. I collapse on the

28

bed. I hold him, kiss his forehead, his nose. He is rigid and cold. I can't understand that. I hear some loud cries, deep like a man's, shrill like a woman's. Who is crying? My husband? My mother-in-law? The nanny, Suchitra? I feel someone's hands on my back, trying to support me – the someone who is crying loudly. I shake them off impatiently. Don't touch me anyone, please! I am still flummoxed by my baby's rigidity. What do you mean, you can't feel me, I am your mother? Where is my baby's softness? Why is his little palm motionless on mine? How can someone three-dimensional feel one-dimensional? Why is it that when breath leaves, the body becomes stiff?

People – neighbours, maids, well-wishers – open the door and look in. I know everyone wants to comfort and hold me when I break down and cry. They are almost waiting for that to happen. I don't. I just want to shut the door and sit here in the cool with him.

You turned eight months today. Your passport was issued today. Two cheques have arrived from unknown kind donors. Only about £2000 of the £100,000 we are trying to raise for your treatment but still, big drops of water in the ocean we need to create. To take you to London so that you can have a bone marrow transplant at Great Ormond Street Hospital. It's the only cure for the condition you have, Severe Combined Immunodeficiency, known as SCID, an acronym that I first heard only a month back, but which will define me forever.

This morning, when I was waving at you just before leaving for work, you stared at me. You were on Suchitra's lap, feeding from your bottle. A stare, such a fixed intense stare, as if you wanted to tell me something.

'What is it, baby?' I asked. Nothing from you. Not a smile, just that look.

Later, I would be convinced that you knew. That you wanted to tell me, 'Hold me, Mummy, just one more time. Once you leave, I can go too.' But I was pushing myself so hard to get to the office, to write to yet another doctor, to count the cheques coming in, to organise whatever I could, that I didn't stop to give you a cuddle.

I stroke his face. I can't believe this is it; the end of my fight, the end of my baby. The bedside table is weighed down with medicines. Tomorrow – we won't have to measure tonics, crush pills. Tomorrow – what were we meant to do?

More people open the door and look inside. I realise they look familiar. They are the colleagues I was with only an hour ago. They too have come to see me, I think. So many people here. I stay sitting on the bed, baby on my lap, and smile at them, as if this is very normal. I don't cry.

'You are taking it so well,' someone says.

How does anyone take something like this? I wonder. People come in and leave quietly. They shut the door, as you do in an air-conditioned room. Outside they are all murmuring and whispering. Someone is offering them a drink, a cup of tea or a glass of water. Perhaps it's Suchitra, the beautiful, caring woman who looked after him like a substitute mother, while I went to work.

Left to myself, I hug him, I smell him. I lie him on the bed gently, go to the drawer and get a pair of scissors. I cut some locks of hair and find a small cloth purse to put them safely in. I sit back on the bed and hold him on my lap again. So hard. He is so stiff, like a piece of wood. I want to shake life into him. I scream silently. 'Are you here somewhere? Do you know my tears? Do you know I loved you?' I had read you need to pray for the dead as they leave and let them go with happiness. I shut my eyes and try to pray, but my shoulders are shaking and my face is wet. 'Stay happy always. Let him go, let him go.'

More people come in. An assortment of neighbours and my husband's colleagues. They tell me they need to take him away. I look at them askance. I thought we could stay this way for as long as I wanted.

I ask them, for I didn't know. 'Is there a…graveyard nearby? Won't you need to make arrangements?' It is easier to ask factual questions in a composed manner almost as if I am meeting a client.

'It's not too far. It's very simple. He will be buried, nothing much to be done.'

'Buried, but why?'

We are Hindus, our dead are cremated. The pure fire licking away at our bodies until they are reduced to ashes, from dust to dust. Even though I have never seen a funeral, I have seen enough Bollywood movies to imagine my baby wrapped in white sheets, covered with flowers, burning on a pyre.

'Hindu cremation rites needn't be done for babies under one,' they explain. 'He has to be buried.' I don't like that. I sit there, insisting there must be a proper cremation. There are no coffins, they say, so he will be buried in a hole in the ground. My baby can't be left like that. They ask my mother-in-law to talk to me. She tries to explain. Adults are cremated on open pyres but not babies, not under one year of age. While people who have lived their lives have to be cremated and their bodies have to perish, babies haven't started their cycle of Karma. Their bodies needn't be burnt. It also means we won't have to observe the rigid twelve day fasts and customs which are normal practice after a cremation. It is so gruelling that it would be better not to have to do that, someone says. 'It will be so much easier if he is buried,' someone

31

else adds. As if inconveniences make any difference to parents who have lost their only child.

The Hindu ways are so esoteric, sometimes so unknown. A baby who hasn't turned one, isn't he a person? But I don't know what else I can do. It's not the way, they all insist in chorus. I am too tired to argue. I don't think of asking anyone or even calling my parents but someone must have told them the news. Someone is surely telling everyone as more and more people arrive. They are calling to offer their condolences. But the people around me seem to be in a hurry and are speaking rapidly to each other. They are perhaps contacting the workers at the graveyard. But why are they in such a blooming hurry? It is only years later I realise that when there's a death, there is haste to remove the body. The person becomes a mere body very quickly. Perhaps it's something to do with the weather and the dread of decomposition in the heat.

When I ask more questions like how long it will take to get to the graveyard, they tell me I can't accompany them. They explain patiently that it's a peaceful burial ground. Really, it is nice, but well, women don't Too grim. I can stay at home and rest. I have never lost anyone I loved, apart from my pet dogs and even then I was at the end only with one of them. The others died in my absence. When my grandmother died, I was busy working in Delhi and didn't come back. I really know nothing about any of this.

'You will take him like that? Just like that?' I ask, but I don't put up a fight when someone, maybe my husband, takes him from my grasp, in his old clothes, wrapped in an orange baby sheet. Hours, days, months, years later, I will still be asking myself why I didn't change him into his new jeans, the nice red, striped t-shirt I had been saving for a time when he would be well enough to go out? Why did I let him go in the mismatched clothes he had gone to bed

in? Why did I let him go? For years, I will have nightmares about him lying under the earth, covered in a sheet, without a coffin, his face gradually being eaten away, clothes and flesh decomposing.

Much later, I will force myself to ask for the details of what happened that day, down to his very last breath.

I will find out that after breakfast, he had seemed to gag.

'You fed him too much,' my mother-in-law had said accusingly to Suchitra.

I will find out how he turned blue, how the security guard had been sent to call a cab, how they had gone to the nearest nursing home and how, on the way there, in the car, safe in Suchitra's arms, he had looked steadily at her for an instant and was gone. Of how they told the nursing home there was no need for a post-mortem. We didn't want to know the exact cause of death. We knew the reason.

I knew they had done their best, I knew he must have felt loved at that moment of passing but the voice in my head laughed at me. It didn't let me forget. For years it raged at me. 'You! You, you, the mother, you couldn't save your own baby and not only that, you weren't even there!'

So for years I will have nightmares of babies dying, of babies suffering and no one being able to help, neither me nor anyone else. For years, I will remember the feeling of holding a baby and a staggering emptiness in my arms.

And for years, I will not be able to bring myself to fill those arms again.

SECTION 2 – GENETICS – SORROW

1

The place is India, the time the late nineties. I was married a few months after I turned twenty-four. This is nothing very unusual. Perhaps I was a bit young but many of my friends were on the brink of matrimony and some celebrating first anniversaries. I graduated as a Telecommunications Engineer, one of five women among two hundred and twenty-five men in my year, then studied for a Master's in Business Administration, a very popular choice. I'd got a job through the campus interviews, worked for a year, and in that year met my husband. It was a whirlwind romance and when I announced I wanted to get married, my parents were secretly relieved. Delhi, where I lived, wasn't the safest place in the world. I flat-shared with two colleagues, both men, in a rather unconventional arrangement. Marriage would bring the much needed security and stability required in any girl's life, especially mine.

So there I was, glowing in a gold-red saree, in front of the sacred fire as the priest chanted Sanskrit mantras to marry us. Our families stood around us. Everyone looked beautiful, smiles flashed. Even the rain Gods must have approved, for it rained, unexpectedly, catching us all unawares. 'Rain in February? It is a lucky omen,' everyone said.

We honeymooned in Goa, then went back to Delhi where we lived and worked. Like so many other newlyweds.

Within a couple of years, there were questions, nudges from relatives, friends, acquaintances. 'When are you giving us some news?' 'Is there any good news yet?' Friends who had married a year or two later were already beginning to share 'news'. I had no such plans. I had wanted to get married in an idealistic dream of love and togetherness but children were far from my thoughts. Within the last two years, I'd changed jobs twice before I found a company where I was content. I wanted to earn my keep, so to speak, and plan for a family at some point in the future. My husband, ever the practical man, saw the sense in that and was supportive. I focussed on building a career.

But apart from the practical issues, the truth was that babies made me nervous. Unlike most girls I knew, including my sister, I'd never been one to coo over cute babies or play much with kids. I didn't feel an urge to become a mother. There was so much else I wanted to do and achieve.

An unmarried colleague was wistfully talking about the babies he would like to have. 'But why do you even want to have a baby?' I asked. 'They are such a hassle!'

'Why? They increase love, they multiply love,' he replied

I didn't see it that way. Still I kept getting 'news.' More births. More questions. Advice that you must have your two kids before you are thirty so you have enough time to enjoy them. Ancient advice, sound advice perhaps. How I disliked the traditional Indian ways and customs. I had never wanted to conform. The more people pressed, the more I questioned. Did a woman have to have children to feel fulfilled? I had chosen to be in sales and my demanding job swallowed my days very effectively.

My rebellion lasted about four years but with my background of doing the right thing at the right time, and with a fair spirit of competition, I was beginning to keel. The norm seemed to be a first child within two years of a marriage and the second three to four years later.

We had moved from Delhi to Kolkata, still called Calcutta by many, after my husband was transferred. At first I had been dismayed at the news. It was the sleepy capital of the East with fewer opportunities than flashy, contemporary Delhi. It was almost a death posting for a young couple trying to further their careers but my husband said it wouldn't be forever and he had often heard of Calcutta opening doors for people. He even joked that it could be a gateway to London. He suggested that the slower pace of the city would be appropriate for starting a family. Friends who knew Calcutta convinced me it wasn't that bad. It was a more convenient place to live, the food was good, and the shopping amazing. My in-laws were delighted because it was much closer to our home state of Odisha. They expected we would visit them every weekend.

I moved with a sinking heart, hoping all these other opinions were right.

2

I could see that Calcutta was different, nowhere near as commercial as Mumbai or Delhi, with a slower pace and a warm heart. I sensed a veil of nostalgia and yearning that hung over the whole city. And yet I was depressed. We lived in Salt Lake City, a newly developed area outside the central old city. A small slum sat right in front of our complex. The maid who came in to clean lived in one of the tenements. From our tiny balcony, I could see right into their homes: the pots over open fires, children playing outside. When we drove to the offices from Salt Lake to central Calcutta, we crossed vast tracts of slums, bare-bodied people everywhere, broken down buses carrying millions across the city. I wasn't a stranger to poverty but somehow in Calcutta it was perpetually in my face.

I had stayed with the same company that had willingly transferred me because they wanted to retain my skills, but the Calcutta office felt like a different enterprise altogether. It was a closed community of Bengalis who spoke a language I couldn't totally understand even though it was close to my mother tongue, Odia. I could see I didn't belong. To add to my woes, my boss was a tyrant. Whereas in Delhi I had some status and a reputation because I'd brought in a very big international client, here I was ordered around as the youngest member of the team. 'Photocopy this. Do that. Fetch this for me.' This was no way to treat someone with an MBA who had been highly thought of. I retaliated, and argued with my boss and the other men, until the only other girl in the team told me her story. She too, like me, had protested until they demoted her, until they reversed her career path. She decided instead to concentrate on having a family. Her daughter was now two years old. In a couple of years, she would be ready for school and the mother ready for a more demanding job. She advised I do the same, use this hiatus for my own benefit, have a baby, and a few years later leave for greener pastures. The plan didn't seem feasible because I could barely get through one day, let alone contemplate spending a year or more in this office while planning a baby. The boss made things unbearable, refusing a promotion and increasingly making me do errands well beneath my skill level. I left within a couple of months.

I joined a small software company. They developed billing software solutions that were sold all over the world and the team of sales and product managers jetsetted around the globe. Soon I was travelling to exotic locations with every month bringing a new destination. I was selling successfully, earning commissions and enjoying every minute of it. But the biological clock was ticking, and I worried. How would a baby fit into my schedule? How would I get back to work after a baby? Would I still be able to travel? But I'd made up my mind. I was well enough established to take a small break.

Within a month of trying to conceive, I had a movie-style fainting fit in the bathroom. A quick visit to the doctor confirmed the pregnancy.

It went well. A perfect, worry-free time. I travelled to South Africa at three months, England at five months. I closed some more contracts. When it was time to go on maternity leave, the

American CEO said, 'Good luck, and if you don't come back to work after your baby, we will understand. Equally, if you do, we will be most happy to have you back.'

'There is no question of not coming back. I will be back in three months,' I said.

'Don't be so hard on yourself,' he said kindly.

Later I realised the western way was often to take it easy, have one, two, three babies. Take a break, come back to work, or not. In the United Kingdom, maternity leave was up to a year, though largely unpaid. In India, however, most of my friends were back at work after the very short maternity leave of three months. You couldn't usually extend it, with or without pay. However, I had a good plan. I would take my three months of leave, then work from home for a month so I would have four months at home with the baby. My friends had told me about specialised agencies who would send in women trained in childcare. They came at 8 a.m. and left at 8 p.m. – a full twelve hours – and charged fifteen hundred Rupees (about fifteen pounds). 'Slightly steep, but worth it,' they said. I would find someone like that. My mother would come and live with us for a few months, and then it would be my mother-in-law's turn. They would keep an eye on the carer and I would get back to my sales and travelling.

My career was my second skin. I would always balance it with family. I had everything planned. Or so I thought.

3

At seven months, the gynaecologist, Dr. Ray, said the scan report showed the baby was lying breech. It meant I would need a Caesarean section. I was disappointed, being all for natural ways, averse to hospitals and operations, despite the many doctors in my family – my grandfather, father, father-in-law and sister.

'But why would you even want to go through all the pain of a normal delivery? A Caesarean is the modern way,' my friend, who had recommended Dr. Ray, said. 'Most of us have had a C-section. It's so much easier!'

The doctors, technicians and nursing homes were an ecosystem. Dr. Ray sent us for scans to another clinic. His patients were admitted to Woodlands, an expensive nursing home in South Calcutta. Most of his patients were under the care of the pediatrician in his own team. We paid separately for all of these services. Since my medical insurance was rather generous, we would be able to afford a single room in Woodlands for my surgery. Friends waxed eloquently about the continental food, the television sets, and the wonderful care I could expect. 'A single room? You'll have such a good time!'

My mother arrived to stay with us for a few months to help once the baby was born. My father-in-law came too and, being a doctor, would be allowed into the operating theatre when the time came, while my husband, the father of the child, would remain outside. My operation was scheduled for the 22nd of October.

It was a drizzly morning. I would later note that all the momentous occasions in my life would be accompanied by rain. Around 8 a.m. I was taken to the operating theatre, nervous but excited. I would have a general anaesthetic rather than an epidural because that was Dr. Ray's preference.

I still remember my first words when I came to.

'Doctor, I'm in agony.' I felt a searing pain. In the place of my wondrous round, big belly, I could feel the harsh cut. A tear in two. An unhealing burn.

'You've just had an operation,' he said. 'It's natural you will be in pain.'

I saw my husband through half-open eyes as I was being wheeled out of the operating theatre into my room.

'A boy,' he smiled at me.

A boy! I had always expected to have a girl. My sister had a son, but I was so sure I would have a little girl. In India, doctors aren't allowed to divulge the gender of the child because of the ongoing practice of female infanticide, not that it prevented some from doing so and then helping abort the child, all for a price. But normally couples didn't know the gender of their baby before the birth.

'A boy! Are you sure?' I asked.

'Very sure,' he laughed.

The anaesthesia caught up with me and I fell asleep. Meanwhile my baby had been taken to the nursery. It was a large room that ran along the length of the corridor, opposite the maternity wards and rooms. Rows and rows of cribs were visible through glass windows. The babies were kept there so the mothers could rest post-delivery. My mother was very surprised at this arrangement.

'It's a western practice,' the nurse told her, 'and it's very effective because the tired mother gets some rest.'

'But babies need to be with their mothers after birth. How can the baby sleep alone?'

'The babies aren't alone,' I explained when my mother looked unconvinced. 'There are other babies and the nurses are looking after them. Besides, Woodlands can't be wrong, can it? It's the best hospital in the city.' I was proud that my hard-earned money was buying all this for me. My company's medical insurance, my efforts, my money, my baby, mine, mine, mine. This was the new modern way and it was correct, I insisted.

I had a long sleep. It was late afternoon when a nurse came in with a little bundle. I remember a red-checked sheet, a squished face, shut eyes and a plump, warm baby placed in my hands. I couldn't sit up with the pain but the nurse was saying, 'Here. You need to feed him.'

'I can't. It's so painful. I can't even sit up.'

'You must try.' Putting him down beside me, she left.

He lay there, a squirming bundle as I held his tiny perfect fingers. On his arm there was a band with a large tag on which was written my room number, his identification. His poor arm was red from the band.

'They should get a little cot and leave him in the room. It's such a big room as it is,' my mother said, yet again. 'Never heard of this. Babies are meant to be with their mothers.'

'But what if I was sharing the room or had been in a ward? Imagine having several babies in one room. They would cry the place down and none of us would be able to rest.'

I was relieved I wasn't expected to manage a baby on my own.

I was already missing my laptop, my calls. I was thinking about a proposal we had submitted to a customer and whether we would be shortlisted or not.

Apart from the excruciating pain in my abdomen, it all seemed so easy. I had done it. I was a mother.

4

He was perfect. But I wasn't. I couldn't cope with the pain nor relax in the apparent luxury everyone had praised. The pain was horrendous. So many of my friends had been through this; why hadn't anyone warned me?

The nurse, meanwhile, was trying to get me to stand and walk to the bathroom, and though I tried to get off the bed, I made no progress. It was impossible to move more than a few inches. She regaled me with stories of so-and-so in the next room who'd had her operation at the same time as me and was walking around in the corridors. And of so-and-so who was discharged within two days because she'd recovered so fast. At the rate I was going, I would be here for a week.

'You have to start walking,' she said. I knew that a 'C-section package' was for five days, all paid, and I had no intention of leaving any sooner. The thought of having to walk up the stairs to our flat on the third floor was frightening.

Dr. Kapoor, the paediatrician visited me soon after the nurse. He was a smallish man with a moustache, a bit like a well-meaning rodent.

'I have just seen your baby,' he cooed. 'He's lovely. Perfect weight, perfect size. And you, how are you?'

'I'm not able to walk. The woman next door is walking. I can't even sit up. It's so painful.' I was distraught. I burst into tears.

'You are still in pain? But aren't you having any pain-killers?'

That's when we realised they had forgotten to give me painkillers. Dr. Ray had contracted malaria the day of my operation. He'd left no instructions and as a result the team of nurses left me to my fate. I hadn't been given any of the famous continental food, or any solid food for that matter. Weak from the operation, it was no wonder I couldn't walk. After consoling me, Dr. Kapoor went and spoke to the nurses. Soon they got me a hot meal.

Later they tried to get me to walk. I managed to get down from the bed and hobble to the bathroom. I was bent double. I will never be whole again, I thought dramatically, not knowing how close to the truth I was. In place of my shining, smooth, round stomach, there was a swollen mass whipped with stretch marks and a large bandage over the cut. It looked and felt ugly. The girl who had walked in happy and confident, discussing a new deal with a colleague in London, felt shrivelled and scarred.

Visiting hours were in the evening. At about six o' clock, the thick blue curtains over the windows facing the corridor, hiding the nursery from view, were drawn back to reveal the rows of babies in their cribs. It was rather like watching animals in a zoo. Parents, relatives and the new mothers stood outside and looked through the viewing panel. My mother, father-in-law and husband would watch our baby and then come back excited to report how he was blissfully asleep, how he looked just like me, no, just like my husband. There were differences of opinion and no consistency in their words.

It was the end of the second day. I lay all evening in bed and didn't attempt to walk to the viewing area.

'Tomorrow, you have to come in the morning for feeding

time,' the nurse warned me. 'So–and–so has done all three feeds today and she had her operation after you. Everyone is walking except you. The longer you leave it, the more it will hurt.'

Feeding time was when the mothers went across to the nursery. The babies were taken out of their cribs, stripped down to their nappies and weighed, squealing and mewling. Then they were handed to their mothers who sat patiently on chairs arranged in rows like in a classroom. A mass feeding began. At the end of the designated fifteen or twenty minutes, the nurses said stop and, one by one, the babies were weighed again. The difference in weight was announced. The baby who had fed the most made for a very proud mother.

I couldn't make the next morning's feeding time, but in the afternoon, thanks to painkillers and having regained a little strength from eating some meals I hobbled along to the feeding room. I took my place next to a buxom woman in a nightgown. She looked very sure of herself. She had done this before. All the women looked confident, waiting to feed, large breasts sometimes already exposed, ready to start the minute the babies were placed in their arms. I had managed to feed him in my bed, though still not able to sit properly and with my mother trying to help the baby latch on. Now I would be doing this on my own. I was terrified.

They handed him to me and I held him close. For the next fifteen minutes, he fed seriously. When they took the babies away and announced the weights, he was the baby with the highest score. The nurses applauded and pointed at me. This was a competition. The buxom women stared at me – the novice mother who couldn't stand properly and didn't look as fertile as them. Meanwhile I was in love with this tiny being who was already on my side. I smiled at him as he was taken back to his crib, promising I would be back for the next feeding time.

When we were discharged after my five days, a wheelchair was brought to take me out to the car park. How was I supposed to walk up the three flights of stairs at home? My baby sat on my mother's lap – car seats were unheard of – and my husband drove us home. I felt the cut would open any minute as I struggled up the stairs.

5

A month passed in a routine of nappies, sleep times, feeding times. My baby was really good and slept for a few hours at a stretch.

I got in touch with childminding agencies and a few women came for interviews. I didn't like most of them. They seemed too aggressive, or too common, or too untidy. I was looking for someone who would work with us long-term. What if I was away for a whole week travelling in another country, would this woman or that one be able to manage my baby? How could I think of leaving my baby all day with someone like this? None inspired my confidence.

After a few rejections, the agency sent a dark, slight woman who, unlike the others who were very sure about the right way to bring up a baby, was soft spoken and looked genuinely happy when she saw my baby.

'I will do everything,' she said. I will cook, clean the house, look after your baby, iron his clothes...'

'It's all right,' I said, 'we have a full time housekeeper as well.'

But still I wasn't sure.

'Suchitra seems nice but she isn't educated,' I said to my husband and mother that evening. 'I was hoping we'd find a proper nanny. I mean she can't speak in English and...'

'I am not sure you'll find educated women wanting to be

nannies,' my mother said. 'Why don't you ask your colleagues or friends? They may know someone.'

'What else did you expect? My nanny is great and she hasn't completed school even! Do you want an English nanny then?' my friend said when I asked.

'This is the best you'll get in India,' other friends confirmed.

'What is the difference between a nanny and a normal maid or cleaner?' I asked

'Nothing, except that she would have some prior experience of managing babies. You need to consider the woman's personality. If she is willing to learn and seems kind…'

I reluctantly agreed, realising I had little option.

I watched Suchitra change his nappy, mix his milk, put him in his cot to sleep. I noted her gentle manner and how he took to her. There were times when I couldn't stop him from crying but she could. In an instant. She would lay him on her shoulder and walk round the small flat, murmuring, babushuna, babushuna[2]. She would sing to him in Bengali until his eyes grew heavy with sleep.

Every month we met Dr. Kapoor who continued to coo in delight as he weighed my baby.

'You are doing so well. Look how healthy he is, all from breast milk,' he would say, encouraging me.

Plump. Growing well. Perfect. He made me so proud. After all, his name, Akshyat, chosen by me, meant 'whole', unhurt in any way.

---

2 Babushuna: a Bengali term of endearment for little boys. Babu a term of respect, and shuna meaning gold or good.

6

I was back at work. We both left around 8.30 a.m. and got home after 7 p.m. In the office, my screensaver flashed pictures of Akshyat from birth. He was around four-and-a-half months. Colleagues stopped at my desk to welcome me back and have a chat.

'He's so cute.

'He looks just like you.'

'He looks more like your husband, isn't it?'

I would smile, the proud mother, and look for myself in his eyes, his mouth, his little nose, his rare smiles.

'The GSMA conference is in Paris in two months time. Do you think you could attend it?' my boss asked me.

'I am sure I can. I will,' I said.

My mother was still with us, and assured it would be all right if I started to wean him from the night time feeds. He was already bottle-fed during the day. I thought about other practical problems. What would I wear? Could I fit back into my navy trousers? Into the black skirt suit?

But the pain around my scar persisted and I still felt cut in two. Later I would wonder if it was a premonition. I called Dr. Ray.

'It's almost four months since the operation. You should feel better by now. Why don't you come and see me?' he suggested.

He checked and confirmed that the cut had completely healed. There was no problem there so I should be feeling fine. I still walked bent over. To get back to my former life, I would have to stand up straighter.

In the months following the birth, I often had a strange experience while asleep. I felt a strong breeze flowing through the room. A great whooshing sound filled the night. If I gave in, if I allowed myself to be swept away, I would soar out of my body and look down at the sleeping forms on the bed. I wouldn't know how to return. I would force my eyes open and everything would feel normal again.

I told my mother.

'Perhaps it is your body remembering the anaesthesia,' she said. 'Next time, that is if there is a next time, keep your eyes shut and pray to The Mother[3]. Recite her name over and over again.'

It happened again a few nights later, a great storm threatening to take me away. My mother's suggestion might have worked but I didn't want to test the power of prayer, and be swept out of my body if it didn't work, so I forced myself awake. I wasn't a religious or spiritual person, nor any kind of a psychic. I couldn't understand why this was happening.

It stopped after a couple of months. Later I wondered if it was a sign, a warning, a premonition about events that would

3 The Mother: Mirra Alfassa, from France, settled in Pondicherry in South India, after she met the revolutionary turned spiritual leader Sri Aurobindo. They set up an ashram in Pondicherry and she is revered as The Mother. My parents believed in their philosophy and accepted them as our spiritual gurus.

dislocate me and force me well outside my familiar life. Years later it would occur again, in a different place, in different circumstances, but always with the same sense of a brewing storm.

The feeling was so intense, I still remember it, although I never understood it.

7

Dr. Kapoor gave us a complex chart of menus. For a week, apple puree should be introduced as the first solid followed by mashed banana for the second week, then a third new food in the third week and so on. I followed it strictly.

'What's the fuss? Haven't we raised babies and fed them solid food before?' my mother-in-law said on the phone.

'He's London educated. This is the modern way. The only baby food you all knew was khichdi[4],' I said.

While you couldn't argue with its nutritional value, I had seen too many friends and relatives stubbornly feed a reluctant baby with spoonfuls of khichdi with the baby equally stubbornly spitting it out.

'Maybe babushuna would like to have some kheer[5]? Shall I make some?' Suchitra asked once.

I consulted the chart. 'According to Dr. Kapoor, rice pudding should only be introduced at five months,' I declared.

I saw my mother and Suchitra suppress smiles, but what did they know? My baby was backed by science, education and refined modern ways, I thought proudly. I would do the best for him and I knew what was best.

---

4 Khichdi: rice, vegetables and lentils cooked together as a balanced one pot meal. Pureed, it is a popular first food for babies

5 Kheer: creamy dessert of milk and rice, rather like a sweet rice pudding

We were getting used to being parents. Our baby was eating well and growing well. I had shaken off the pain and was walking straighter. When he was four-and-a-half months old, I planned a first evening out with my colleagues. All dressed up in a red salwar kameez, I held him up, my chubby baby in his new yellow outfit, and we posed for a picture. I held him in my arms, my eyes on his face. A perfect moment, but that was the last.

That night, spots appeared all over his body – on his hands, legs, trunk and face. The next day he developed a fever, first it came in the evenings, then in the day, soon all day and all night. It was calmed by Calpol but only for a few hours and always it returned in full fury. And when it came, he would stop eating. Sometimes he would throw up. White milk in a projectile landed on my clothes in the middle of the night. There was another worry. The site of the BCG vaccine on his left arm was a swollen white lump.

'This is the way it's meant to be,' Dr. Kapoor told us. 'Don't worry, he's only reacting to the BCG. It's a slightly delayed reaction, it happens at four months, but because he had the vaccine at one month, not at birth like most, this is normal.'

'But what about the rash? What about the fever?' we asked. New parents in a panic, watching a suddenly afflicted baby.

'The fever…well, he's just got fever like babies sometimes do. The rash, let's see…I think…I think it might be scabies.'

Scabies? That itchy, messy, skin condition? We are a modern, nuclear family who are careful with our children. Scabies? That's what children who don't wash and play on streets get.

'How can my baby get scabies?' I was incensed.

'You know, you have this babysitter, I mean these people, they live in slums. You don't know what they carry. Tell her to wash her hands, to remain clean. Use this lotion, soon he will be well.'

Silently I protested but said nothing. Suchitra couldn't be the reason because she took all possible precautions. We paid Dr. Kapoor his usual consultation fee of Rs.250[6] and were told to come back in two weeks.

The thick creamy lotion didn't help. The rash and fever grew. The huge white swelling on the vaccine site burst just as Dr. Kapoor predicted. But in its place there was a hollowed out area which grew deeper, like a pit.

'Shouldn't this fill up?' we asked, visiting him again two days later.

This time, Dr. Kapoor looked a bit worried. He was only a paediatrician, he said. This was some sort of a skin disorder which a skin doctor would know more about. He referred us to Dr. Dhar, a specialist in his ecosystem.

The next evening, we went to Dr. Dhar's clinic in another part of the city. We had to wait our turn. Akshyat moaned as he lay on my lap.

'All these visits are disturbing his routine,' I complained to my husband. 'It's almost dinner time. I wish these doctors could find out what is wrong and quickly! Really annoying.'

There was nothing we could do. We had to wait, along with the million others waiting to see the doctor.

Dr. Dhar, a young man with an open face and a large moustache, concluded that not only was it scabies, but also a reaction to scabies. *Scabies* + *a reaction to scabies*, he wrote on the report. He was triumphant in his diagnosis.

'It's rare, but it can happen sometimes,' he said.

He sent us back with anti-allergen medicines. It would all

---

6   Rs 250 is equivalent to £3.00

subside soon, he was sure. We were to come back in two or three days if it hadn't healed.

We went back. The rash was still burning red all over his body. My father-in-law arrived on the overnight train. Their first grandson, their only grandson. This baby meant a lot to the somewhat patriarchal family I had married into. He often accompanied us on our visits to doctors.

'She, the mother, needs to travel to Paris in two weeks. Can she go? Will the child be better?' he asked Dr. Dhar when we went to meet him for the fourth time.

'Yes, I am sure he will be.' Dr. Dhar looked worried as well. Akshyat moaned when the doctor felt his little body.

'Why isn't the site of the vaccine healing?' we asked.

The vaccine site was what they were all glossing over. The skin around its edges was jagged and it was huge, as if someone had dug out some of the flesh from my baby's arm.

'What did the paediatrician have to say about this?' Dr. Dhar asked, his voice accusing. 'I can only comment about the skin rash. Dr. Kapoor needs to treat this.'

'He sent us to you. He said a skin specialist should be able to explain because it's a skin condition and that's why he has a temperature.' We parroted Dr. Kapoor's words.

Forced to make a new diagnosis, Dr. Dhar sent us back with a new label, erythema multiforme, a condition when the body reacts to medication. With that he explained away the rash and temperature. The vaccine wasn't his responsibility.

'I cannot accept payment from another doctor,' he said, when my father-in-law offered it. Dr. Dhar had already showed his respect for his seniority and experience.

'No, we insist. Her insurance will pay us back for these visits!'

my husband and father-in-law said. Both sides perhaps thought there would be no more visits and a diagnosis was found. The fees of one visit didn't make a big difference.

Back home, I searched online and read about erythema multiforme and the Steven Johnson's Syndrome. The pictures looked frightening. I couldn't believe my baby could have such a condition.

The medicines didn't work. The rash remained red and the pit got deeper.

One of my colleagues used her connections to get me an appointment with one of the best skin doctors in the city, Dr. Lath. He had waiting lists up to six months so one needed to have contacts in high places to be seen by him. We went to his clinic in the evening, after work. Surely this doctor would be able to tell us what was wrong.

I remember a dimly lit examining room. I remember the spectacled, bearded doctor in a white shirt. I remember the sudden anguish, almost horror on his face as he looked at my baby, such a beautiful, baby, big for his age, but with the blight of a rash searing his body.

'I don't know what to tell you. Such a young mother. I just don't know what could be wrong,' the doctor said.

'They told us it was scabies, then a reaction to scabies, then erythema multiforme. Could it be any of those?'

'I just don't know. I am so sorry.' He refused to make any diagnosis.

We left, not knowing what to think. What was wrong with these doctors and why couldn't they diagnose something as simple as a rash on a baby?

By now, I was used to reaching out in the night to touch

my baby, who slept next to me, and feel the familiar heat.

'It's coming back,' I would nudge my husband awake.

The lights on, the thermometer in his mouth, the Calpol he would dutifully drink without any protest and, after some time, the body turning cooler to my touch. We would then sleep, only for the fever to return a few hours later.

We didn't know what to do except go back to one of the doctors and since Dr. Kapoor was proving no use, we latched on to Dr. Dhar. At least he seemed committed to help us find an answer. He used some of his contacts and got us an appointment with an even more renowned doctor.

'Dr. Roy is the most respected skin doctor in Calcutta. He's my mentor. People go to him from all parts of the country. If anyone can know for sure what is wrong, it will be him.'

Our appointment was at nine in the evening in the doctor's clinic. These doctors had ferociously busy practices for sure. My father-in-law and mother came with us.

'In all my forty years of practice, I have never seen anything like this,' Dr. Roy said. My gently moaning baby stripped to his nappy lay on the examining table. We repeated the various diagnoses the other doctors had suggested.

'I am sure it's none of those. I would know if it was,' the doctor said.

'If it isn't scabies, a reaction to scabies, or erythema simplex or erythema multiforme, then what is it?'

'That's the problem. I can only tell you what it is not, not what it is. I don't know. I've never seen symptoms like this in my entire career. I think you need to go to a paediatrician. Skin doctors don't have the expertise to deal with something like this.'

He offered no further help. We left, confused and desperately anxious.

We were tired and harassed. Our parents offered us their unconditional support but the strain of having them with us was telling. Every time we consulted a doctor, my father-in-law explained how in 1968 my parents had lost their first born son at the age of six months after recurring unexplained illnesses. None of the doctors we spoke to considered or commented on this piece of information. It would turn out to be vital.

When we returned home that evening, really perplexed at the doctor's reaction, my mother asked, 'Why does your father-in-law keep talking about the boy we lost? Does he have to keep reminding me of my pain? The doctors couldn't cure him and now it's like history repeating itself. They can't find out what's wrong with my grandson either.' I saw tears well up in her eyes.

My parents had never spoken much about their loss. We knew in hazy details the story of how our brother kept falling ill, and how the doctors were not able to offer a diagnosis. They lived in Burla, a small university town in Odisha, and my mother blamed her baby's death on the incompetence of the doctors.

I had no idea why my father-in-law kept telling the doctors the same story. I thought it just one of those weird things in-laws did.

'Let us take Akshyat somewhere else,' my mother said. 'When my son fell ill, we ran from doctor to doctor and no one could help. No one knew what was wrong. You have the resources, you can go somewhere else, maybe Mumbai or Delhi. We couldn't do that for our son, but you must!' She held Akshyat in her arms and wept.

Take him somewhere else? We were comfortable at home. We

had a well-established routine. Meals were produced on time. He had Suchitra to look after him. Where else would we go? We were in contact with so many doctors. Surely one of them would offer us a diagnosis? My mother was overreacting. The story of her baby and mine were different. We were in Calcutta, not Burla. We were going to the best, most expensive doctors in the city. It was just a matter of time and they would figure it out.

We went back to Dr. Dhar. He prescribed steroids. Within a day, the rash had vanished, the fever cleared. I was jubilant.

'The steroids worked! He is getting better.' I was immediately on the phone to Dr. Dhar, telling him that my baby's face was clear of the large red bumps. He was sleeping contentedly. But Dr. Dhar sounded subdued,

'That's good he's better but what can this disease be which responds to steroids but to nothing else? He didn't respond to the antibiotics…it's strange.'

I didn't understand his worry. The red spots seemed to be disappearing, though they had left their marks on his pale skin. I would have to find some anti-blemish cream to clear his skin.

That was my only worry, when three days later, the rash came back. I phoned my sister, a doctor in one of the leading hospitals in Chennai with the update.

'Listen, I have told you before. The medical care in Calcutta is bad. Those doctors aren't able to find out what's wrong and babies can deteriorate fast. You have to act quickly. Come here and admit him to my hospital.'

'We are running from pillar to post consulting all these doctors, spending all this money,' I protested. 'We can't rush to the other end of the country and admit him to a hospital in the south. His home is here.'

How could we let go of everything to go to a different hospital in an unknown city and besides, did I want my poor baby admitted as a patient? The doctors here would just have to use their brains, I thought angrily. But my mother agreed with my sister and was convinced we would get no answers in Calcutta.

Next time we visited Dr. Dhar, he suggested we should consult a Dr. Raychaudhuri.

'He's the best paediatrician in the city. He should be able to help. I don't understand why the baby is responding to steroids and nothing else. I am really worried,' he said.

8

Suchitra insisted on coming this time. She was protective of her babushuna, imagining by being there, she would somehow help in finding the answers. It was afternoon and the heat hung in the air, almost solid to touch. The retinue of my mother, father-in-law, husband, Suchitra, baby and myself went in our small white Maruti car, the loyal steed.

Dr. Raychaudhuri, a dark, stern looking man, looked at baby as he lay on the examining table, moaning.

'He has a big stomach,' he said.

I suppressed a smile. 'He does like to eat. Even when he has fever, he eats so well,' I said with pride.

He looked at me, scorn in his eyes.

'How can you, as a mother, not even realise that his liver is swollen, his spleen is enlarged? Look, place your hands here on his stomach. Have you ever felt this?' I held my hand tentatively on the spot he pointed to. My baby groaned louder.

'That's his liver and its swollen! Why do you think he is making this groaning noise?'

'He has a temperature, that's why. He's had it for months…'

'He is crying because it's painful to touch,' the doctor interrupted. 'If this child was in the west, he would be in hospital! He is seriously ill! Admit him to my nursing home today and I will run some tests to find out what is wrong. This child is not a normal child.'

He started writing a list and I watched his pen curl words on the paper: *blood test, open liver biopsy, bone marrow biopsy, X-Ray. Diagnosis – AIDS? Leukaemia? Autoimmune disorder?'*

'How long will he have to stay here for?' one of us asked.

'I don't know that. Just come and admit him this evening. We will have to run all these tests and find out what's wrong with him.'

There were tears in my eyes and fury in my heart as we walked away from his clinic. His callous manner rankled.

'Whatever I do, I am not admitting my baby in this death trap,' I shouted.

'But he needs to have the tests,' my mother said gently. 'We can't just let him suffer. We have to know what's wrong.'

'Anywhere but here.' I knew I was shouting. 'I hate this stupid man. I hate him. Stupid ugly doctor!' My language often regressed to a spoilt teenager's when my mother was around.

'But he was only trying to help.'

'I hate this heat, the dust, this stupid city. My complete sense of helplessness in this stupid city! Anywhere but here.'

We were silent on the drive back. This was more serious than we could ever have imagined. A doctor had told us directly that they couldn't second-guess anything, they needed to carry out real tests. Even though I disliked him, he had done us a favour. Finally, we had to accept there was something very wrong with our perfect baby.

We had lost our confidence in the Calcutta medical system. The centres of medical excellence were elsewhere. One could either go to the private, corporate hospitals like Apollo which offered a clean environment, well-trained doctors with brilliant infrastructure, or government hospitals like AIIMS in Delhi or CMC (Christian Medical College) in Vellore, teaching hospitals, with a strong focus on medical research.

We narrowed it down to CMC Vellore since my father in-law was able to make the arrangements through a relative. My parents and sister lived in Chennai, close enough to Vellore. It seemed a better choice than Delhi. CMC had a brilliant reputation, and if there was one place in India where we would get some answers for sure, it was there.

Long back, in second grade, we'd read a story about the 'doctor in a wheelchair,' a young woman surgeon who was crippled but worked in CMC and performed complex operations. With the idealism that children are prone to, I had thought I would become a doctor and visit this hospital one day. I never imagined that my idle wish would come true.

Be careful what you wish for, I thought as I called the office travel desk to change my flight from Calcutta – Delhi – Paris, to Calcutta – Chennai, with an open return.

We reached Chennai in the evening. After a car journey of a few hours, CMC loomed in front of us, a low building, dimly lit.

The heat was palpable, even though it was late in the night in April. It was a sign of the hellish days ahead.

My mother, baby and I waited in the paediatric emergency ward while the papers were processed by my husband and father-in-law. The state of disrepair of the ward was horrific with children of different ages and sizes sleeping on rough-looking beds. Drips in arms, casts on legs, faces in bandages – I tried to shield my baby from the awful scene. He must have known he was not in his house, but not understanding, moaned his gentle familiar moan. His body was hot. The fever hardly left him these days. Calpol served no purpose.

'We will die if we have to spend all night here,' I told my mother.

She was speechless. She had been away from her home for months now, though my father was geographically closer now we were in Vellore. She was reliving a past she had put behind her and had tried to forget.

We were soon moved to the 'most expensive' room in the hospital. It was large with no air-conditioning, despite the extreme heat. There was one basic single bed. My mother would have to sleep on the concrete floor on a mat, while my father-in-law and husband would share a room in a guesthouse arranged by their relative.

Within the next couple of hours, they carried out several tests including a chest X-Ray on my tired, crying baby. The team was efficient, the processes in place. Then the nurse took him away saying I mustn't follow. When they brought him back, still crying, a thin tube and bandage was stuck on his little foot.

'What is this?'

'It's called a cannula.'

'But why? And why didn't you tell me you were about to do this?' I asked, furious.

The nurse looked at me blankly, either never having been questioned or never having been asked that question.

'And how long will it need to stay on?' I asked, holding my still-crying baby.

'As long as he is here.'

'And how long will we be here?'

I didn't receive an answer, but she touched my arm quickly, gave me a kindly smile and left.

9

In the morning, the paediatrician, Dr. Verghese, arrived with his group of students. He was a tall, dignified-looking man. I felt reassured just looking at him. Whatever he would tell us, it would surely not be as bad as that doctor in Calcutta.

He started by going over the pieces of the puzzle – the rash, the pit on the vaccine site, a fever that subsided briefly and came back, the swollen liver and, very importantly, the fact that my mother had lost her six-month baby boy from recurring illnesses. When you added all that together and looked for a connection, it pointed very simply at something: a possible genetic disorder which ran in the family and affected immunity. He had a name for it. The words were chilling and incomprehensible: Severe Combined Immuno-deficiency (SCID).

'SCID is a primary immune deficiency,' he told us. 'It's a condition one is born with, when the main white blood cells of the body, which are called the T-and B-cells, don't function. The B-cells help defend and ensure we don't contract an infection. If we do, then it's the T-cells which come into action and fight the infection. When both the T-and B-cells don't work, the body is defenceless. One can catch any infection and not be able to fight it. So even a common cold can be fatal because the cold virus will keep multiplying and spreading. What I suspect has happened to your baby is that the BCG vaccine, which is given to protect against tuberculosis, has given him tuberculosis.'

'But what kind of a vaccine is that, which can create an illness?' I exclaimed.

My father-in-law was against most vaccines, especially the BCG. He had made sure Akshyat wasn't vaccinated at birth. He said vaccines often didn't work. We weren't happy with that decision. It was normal procedure, I had argued. So Akshyat was vaccinated a bit later, when he was a month old. When the pit hadn't healed, he wondered if the vaccine had been corrupt, though Dr. Kapoor had vehemently denied any such possibility. I had imagined Vellore would confirm a contaminated vaccine.

'It's a live vaccine. Most vaccines are killed organisms but in some, a small dose of live bacteria is injected into the body. The body then produces antibodies and you are effectively immunised against the disease. In your baby's case, his non-functioning B-cells couldn't produce any antibodies so he contracted tuberculosis. His T-cells are non-existent so he couldn't fight it. In SCID, the symptoms don't present as in a normal person. Hence, the tuberculosis has shown itself in bizarre ways and has possibly spread to his spine, liver and spleen. The lungs are badly affected already.'

We looked back at our baby who was sleeping quietly, with some respite from pain thanks to the medication. He was being given antibiotics in a drip, straight into the bloodstream to be more effective. This would be done for a week, if not more.

Dr. Verghese had more to say. 'There are several forms of SCID. I can't get it tested here or in fact in any other hospital in India, but I am sure this is a case of X-SCID. In X-SCID, the mother carries a defective X chromosome. If she has a girl

70

and passes the defective X, there is no problem as there is a backup X in the female XX genetic code. If she has a boy, and passes the defective X, the result is fatal because a boy has no backup X in the male XY genetic code. Therefore, with any future pregnancy, there is a one in four possibility of a child having X-SCID. If you have a boy again, there is a fifty percent chance he could have SCID. Unfortunately, you can do nothing to ensure a positive result.'

We could do nothing to ensure the good X was passed on. The result was out of our control. The outcome was written without our consent.

Like a roll of the dice.

It was hard to comprehend. I recalled childhood Biology lessons, a picture of chromosomes. Very vaguely, I remembered some diseases which affected only boys. Had we ever been taught about SCID? Never mind us, were doctors taught? If so, why had none of them guessed this was the problem?

Dr. Verghese looked at my mother. 'So your son probably had SCID as well.'

'His mouth was full of thrush. He had severe diarrhoea. It never went away,' my mother said. Years of not knowing, wondering what had happened, and now this.

'Classic signs of SCID are thrush, reaction to vaccines like BCG, diarrhoea.' Dr. Verghese was now talking to his students who were taking notes. 'We say it is a rare condition with an occurrence of one in a hundred thousand babies but we don't know how many children die from a lack of diagnosis. The problem is that the symptoms are so varied. It could be anything, so you mainly have to watch out for recurring illnesses which don't respond to antibiotics. Only steroids work briefly.'

'But what is the treatment for SCID?' I asked, thinking that was all we needed to know. Never mind about future pregnancies. That's the last thing I was thinking about.

The group seemed to draw in a communal breath. The doctor looked at me for a while before answering. 'The only treatment is a bone marrow transplant but we don't offer that in India. Basically, we can't treat SCID.'

When he was explaining, it sounded like a simple condition so I expected a simple solution. A magic potion to drink and recover? An injection to produce T and B-cells?

'Had it been another type of SCID, ADA-SCID, we could have managed for some years, ordering special enzyme injections from America. In fact, I will send a sample out to my colleague, Dr. Hershfield, in the US just to rule out ADA. But as I said, with the blood test results, the family history, I am ninety-nine-point-nine per cent sure it is X-SCID.'

'So you won't be able to cure him?' I asked dumbly.

'We will treat him and try to cure him of all the current infections. He will also need a long course of drugs for tuberculosis.' This was an illness glamourised in movies with film stars demurely coughing and recuperating in sanatoriums. For my baby to get tuberculosis, the world had been swept from under my feet.

'But the treatment we offer is temporary. He will succumb to something else unless he receives a bone marrow transplant. If there was a sibling, maybe we could have attempted a transplant. But now, your only way out, if you can, is to go abroad. Leave India. Leave this country. That is the only hope.'

'But where? Where abroad?'

'There's no centre in Asia unfortunately. It has to be America.

Or possibly somewhere in Europe. I will also arrange a meeting with the haematologist and he can give you some more information. I will be back tomorrow.'

My perfect baby was defenceless. My country offered us no hope.

Before we came to Vellore, in our Calcutta home, my father-in-law had spent days sitting on the sofa, head in his hands, while we all fretted and planned yet another visit to a doctor. I once got annoyed. 'Why does he think this is the end of the world? Why does he act as if something awful has happened to my baby? We just need to find a good doctor. And why doesn't he know what's wrong, being a doctor himself?' He sat quietly, not even reacting to my shouting, my anger and accusations, worrying, perhaps knowing in his heart that something was very wrong. Something was so wrong that it couldn't ever be set right again.

In the Vellore hospital, I had seen a two-year-old girl in one of the wards being carried by her mother. She had leukaemia and after her third round of chemotherapy was left with no hair and hollow cheeks. Her limbs were skeletal, her eyes stark. I felt sorry for the mother. My baby, in spite of the rash, the fever, still looked healthy enough with his round face, his chubby little arms. Now they were telling me nothing could be done for him?

From scabies, to erythema multiforme to erythema nodosum to leukaemia to liver problems to SCID. Each time the diagnosis worsened. This was not a sentence we could bear.

Blood hums and makes its way through generations. The complex chromosome mapping citing the colour of eyes, the height, the shape of limbs, the way you hold your hand under your chin, the way you tilt your face just like your grandfather! The pattern mapped in the hum of blood. The story of the chromosomes speaking their own language, indecipherable, the story written and ordained.

10

Later, in the internet booth outside the hospital, I emailed my boss in England to tell him I needed to be off work and had no idea for how long. His response was immediate and positive. He told me not to worry about the office. He sent some links to the Great Ormond Street Hospital and Anthony Nolan Bone Marrow Trust. There is treatment elsewhere in the world. Take heart, he wrote.

The shop was freezing cold with the air-conditioning and a fan blowing a cool breeze on my hair. Those few minutes in the booth, away from the heat and the despair of the hospital reminded me of the time that once was, of the person that used to be me. Emailing work reminded me that there was something else I could do instead of being the helpless mother who could only watch her precious child waste away.

But once back in the ward, the other story played on. I was the young, devastated mother everyone felt sorry for. The mother who couldn't make her son better.

We had an appointment with the haematologist the next day. My father-in-law and I walked to the other end of the hospital where his office was.

Dr. Chandi explained about immune deficiencies and primary immune deficiencies. SCID was the most severe. The king of them all. While the hospital routinely carried out bone marrow transplants for leukaemia, they had no expertise with SCID. The complexity of the condition and the complete isolation needed by the patient made it impossible. Later, I would find out that a hapless couple had insisted that their daughter, with an unknown form of SCID, was treated. She died days after the transplant, her body raging with reaction and infections. Dr. Verghese, Dr. Chandi and their teams had been able to do nothing. Now they did not dare to attempt another bone marrow transplant, fearing the outcome would be the same.

'But what about other hospitals in India? AIIMS in Delhi? Jaslok in Bombay?' my father-in-law asked.

'No, not one of them. We are not equipped, nor do we have the experience. If you can, go abroad,' he said. 'America. Or Germany.'

'England?' I asked.

'London…yes London as well. There are some other centres in Europe. Germany, where I was, is one of the best. But if I were you, I would give up. The child is very unwell. The treatment is extremely expensive. Very few can raise the kind of money needed to go abroad for such a long treatment process.'

'We can go abroad,' my father-in-law said quietly. 'My younger son lives in America.' He pointed at me. 'She works for an international company and travels abroad regularly. We came to you because Dr. Verghese said you could advise us about treatment centres.'

'Germany,' he said again.

'Germany isn't much of an option. Maybe London or America,' I said. My company had offices in both places but we didn't deal with Germany.

'It is extremely difficult. My advice would be to give up…it is too expensive a process,' he repeated.

'We can go anywhere we need to.' A dignified man, my father-in-law rarely lost his temper. 'We will do anything we can to treat our child.'

The doctor didn't look convinced. He shrugged, wished us luck and said goodbye. Maybe it was his duty to tell us the worst.

We walked back through the dusty grounds of the hospital. It was midday. The heat was numbing. It rose in waves around us. It burnt through our skin and scorched deep inside. You couldn't escape the heat. You couldn't hide anywhere.

'What a stupid man! Stupid, stupid doctor!' I said, tears hot in my eyes.

What did he know? We would go abroad. We would do anything to save our child. What did he know? We would not give up on our child. We would not!

My thoughts were furious and fast, like my tears.

11

We stayed in Vellore for almost a month.

Apart from everything else, the food was hard to get used to. Vellore is deep in the state of Tamil Nadu and the local food tends to be mostly vegetarian food, spicy dosas, idlis, rasam, sambhar. It was the kind of food we enjoyed once in a while, and in fact dosas used to be a treat. But having this cuisine day in and day out, bought from the roadside restaurants, was taking its toll. In Odisha, our coastal state, the diet was healthy and balanced with rice, vegetables and protein in the form of fish or goat meat or chicken. In Calcutta, West Bengal, it was fairly similar and fish was integral. All of us missed eating our nourishing meals. The watery, spicy curries here, especially in the extreme heat, added to our general sense of despair.

In those days, Pampers and Johnsons hadn't made their way to India in a big way. The nappies available were expensive and poor quality. We used cloth nappies made at home from old sarees and other soft material and had to wash them in the bathroom under the tap, and dry them indoors. Sitting in the bare room, my mother and I felt we had regressed to village life and were living a slum-like existence. I thought of what Suchitra would say, seeing her beloved babushuna on a constant drip of medication, my mother and me washing clothes in a tin bucket, washing his bottles in the kitchen, work which she, like so many of the serving class, would never allow their employers to do.

I started to look forward to the nights when my baby wouldn't fall asleep and would play instead. Finally, free of all the pain he must have endured for months, thanks to the strong medication, he moved his legs and arms freely. He chuckled when I tickled him. I would watch him, enjoying those moments until the round of treatment started all over again – doctors, injections and drugs. It was the only time I had with him, one to one, without Suchitra, or without my preoccupation with work.

Some friends from Chennai came to visit us in the hospital. They looked nervous at first but when they saw our baby's cheerful face and his ready smile, they smiled too.

'He will be fine. Look at him! We wouldn't know he was not well, if you hadn't told us.' They left reassured, thinking maybe we were exaggerating the problem and that there was a cure. People invented alternative scenarios and decided that his immune system would reconstitute itself, that as he grew older and stronger, he would be able to fight the infections.

We knew he couldn't. He didn't have the building blocks to mount a response to any kind of illness. I wanted to say this directly but somehow the confidence of others was a relief to us. For a while we could delude ourselves that things would be fine. We were in hospital and would leave once our treatment was complete.

My husband would bring us our lunch from the small restaurants near the hospital or the guesthouse. They served exactly the same fare, so it didn't make any difference where he got it from. Then, my mother and I would go to the guesthouse for an afternoon nap in the cool air-conditioned room away from the incredible heat. We tried to recoup in that hour or two.

One day, my husband suggested we return a bit later and take a longer rest. 'You must be so tired,' he said.

'Are you sure? Can you manage?'

'Yes, sure, why not? Have a rest.'

When we returned, my husband and father-in-law looked sheepish, as if something had happened. When the nurse put my baby in my arms, I felt a huge bandage on his back, like a paper swan. They told me he had been taken for a bone marrow biopsy. Since it was a painful procedure, everyone decided it would be easier for me not to know. I would have been upset, they said.

'It will hurt a little, for a few days maybe,' the nurse said. 'Hold him carefully.'

There was nothing I could do. Nothing to help the little child we had brought into the world. The room was oppressive. There was nowhere to cry, nowhere to run. I had to wait for the day to finish, for the years to pass, for complete silence until I could cry my heart out.

12

We were discharged when all his infections cleared up with IV antibiotics. The tuberculosis required a longer treatment with oral medication. Dr. Verghese suggested we should try getting some infusions of immunoglobulins (IVIG) at the local hospital which would help keep his immune levels up. This was like a blood transfusion but with plasma cells instead of red blood cells.

At home, our focus would be on keeping him well and infection free, and simultaneously we would prepare to go abroad for treatment. I had written to my boss, and he was already speaking to the CEO to check options for my relocation.

Our flight back was so different from the inbound one. Our baby was free of fever and looked around in wonder, registering the different shapes and colours. His happiness was more heart-rending because we didn't know what we were taking him back to. We were parents who dreaded betraying our child's trust. Briefly, we tried to delude ourselves that nothing was wrong and we were young parents with a normal child. Everything was fine.

Once home, and with my core support system, the internet, at my disposal, I googled SCID. The first site which came up was a support group.

Send an email with the subject line JOIN if your life is affected by SCID, it gently urged. I immediately wrote a few lines about our situation and sent it off, not knowing what to expect. Little did I know that I had just found my life support for many years to come. Little did I know that I would be truly understood by people all over the world even if I had never met them and never would. My virtual family would hold and support me. My virtual family would console me over and over again.

In just a few hours, there were several responses, mostly from mothers in America. Messages of welcome, hope, sympathy and courage. The woman who set up the site and founded the group told me about another family from India who had lost their first child, and when their second daughter was also diagnosed with SCID, had flown to London for treatment. It was the same case I had heard about in Vellore when the doctors had attempted a transplant and it had failed. There were other stories; of children who had been diagnosed after falling unwell repeatedly, of children who were cured after a bone marrow transplant, of children who hadn't survived the transplant or died before it could take place. The messages came with a warning – a child with SCID rarely makes it to their first birthday without treatment.

My baby was seven months old. The walls were closing in on us.

They sent me a list of treatment centres all over the world. A few in America and a few in Europe – London, Paris, Italy. No one had details of a centre in Germany despite what the haematologist had told us. I wrote to every doctor, each highly skilled, respected, revered, famous. Each wrote back promptly, with empathy and some hard facts.

Dr. Jones wrote back from Great Ormond Street hospital in London saying the estimated cost of treatment would be around a hundred thousand pounds. The reason for the astronomical expense was that the child had to be first cleared of all infections, then kept in complete isolation in specially filtered rooms. It also took time to find a well-matched donor and following the transplant, adverse reactions would have to be monitored. All this meant a lengthy hospital stay. The most recommended hospital in America was Duke University in North Carolina, thanks to a wonderful doctor who had developed a non-invasive form of treatment without chemotherapy. She responded to my mail within an hour. The cost, she stated, was similar, around two hundred and fifty thousand dollars. The doctor from Necker hospital in Paris emailed that they dissuaded parents from outside Europe coming for treatment because after the transplant, it was necessary to remain in the country for regular hospital check-ups. It wasn't a simple matter of let's have an operation and leave. This was treatment for life. Where would we stay for such a long period? St Jude in Memphis, USA offered free treatment but they wrote back to say frankly the waiting list was already long and preference would be given to American patients.

While my husband's family explored options in America, for me the way was clear. I reported to the European office in London. I managed the African sales region even though I was based in India. There had been talk of moving me to the office in England before my pregnancy but I hadn't been very keen then. But what if they could move me to London now? My husband had an MBA in Finance and London was the financial capital of the world. England was one of the few countries which allowed the spouse to work without additional permits.

'He will find a job in a few months,' my friend in England told me encouragingly. 'Once you are settled here and paying your taxes, you will be under the National Health. They will recognise this is a critical case.' He went on to tell me about the NHS.

I lived in a country where people could die from lack of treatment, where families sold homes to afford hospital bills. I thought my friend was pulling my leg about a country where medical treatment was free for residents.

'So all you need to do now is move to the London office. Talk to the head, talk to everyone. They like you. You have worked so hard for the company. Tell them they have to move you to London. Raise the money and the initial treatment can start immediately under private care. Since he will need to be monitored for years, things will be simpler if you are living here.'

It sounded like a plan.

'But how will you raise such an astronomical amount?' my aunt asked. She had come to support us now that my mother had left.

'Small drops make an ocean,' I said, trying to portray an optimism I didn't feel. 'People will donate for a cause. The amount – a hundred thousand pounds in cash (and this was in 1999) – was etched in my mind and every day I wondered how would we ever raise it.

For years after, I will think of it, for years I will measure life against a hundred thousand pounds.

My uncle came to meet us, complete with a list of our relatives who would donate and how much. My husband was talking about selling his share in his father's property. My parents offered to sell their house. All generous offers, yet they weren't enough. The family who had taken their daughter to the UK for treatment said that the Indian population in England had responded very generously when they appealed on Sunrise Radio.

'They love children here,' she told me.

We planned a global fundraising campaign. We would reach out to friends and family who in turn would reach out to their contacts.

I called Dr. Kapoor and told him about the diagnosis and our plans to go to London. 'Come and meet me. I will tell you everything you need to know about the hospital. I lived in London for a while, you know.'

My husband asked if Dr. Kapoor would prove useful at all, but since he had offered to help, I thought we should go. We went without our baby.

'The doctors in Great Ormond are good, but you know what? The hospital doesn't look at all impressive. Don't go by what you see,' he advised. He gave us some suggestions about nutrition, with me wondering if he actually understood the magnitude of SCID. I was expecting an apology for his failure to give us a diagnosis. And not only for himself but on behalf of the dozen other doctors we had consulted in Calcutta who had no clue either. He wasn't at all contrite. Outside, he waited until my husband handed him his fees of two hundred and fifty Rupees.

'He still asks for money when he knows we are trying to raise a hundred thousand pounds!! And he knows nothing! I know more about SCID and the transplant process from my friends in the support group,' I muttered angrily when we left. 'What a man! Hope we never see him again.'

'He did look after our baby well enough before the problems started,' my husband replied.

I looked at him so furiously, he didn't dare say another word.

'This whole city is full of commercially-minded, foolish doctors who have no clue how to treat anyone.'

'Why this city? This whole country,' he said.

It was ironic that we felt this way when both our fathers were doctors.

We drafted an email explaining SCID and why we needed to fundraise and sent it to our friends asking them to circulate it in their social and business networks with a note that our plea was genuine. Those were the days before social media. Had there been Facebook and WhatsApp and Twitter, the results would surely have been quicker, yet even then, within a couple of days, incredibly, cheques started coming in. Generous donations from complete strangers. My cousin in Paris had circulated the email within his company and one of his colleagues from India sent us a lakh of Rupees, the equivalent of about a thousand pounds. My friend's boss sent in Rupees twenty-five thousand, equivalent to two hundred and fifty pounds. We'd established four collection points – my cousin in America, my cousin in Paris, my friend in England, and us in India because we hoped contributions would be global. Friends got in touch, some apologising they could contribute only a little, some not asking any questions and giving with their hearts. The support was overwhelming.

And years later, much later, sitting in my quiet London home, I would, one day somehow chance across the same email on the website indiadivine.org, not knowing who placed it there, who was the kind person vouching this was a genuine case and asking people to donate. It had been put up on 19th June 2000.

Dear friend,

We are desperate to save our baby boy Akshyat (7.5 months old) from a fatal condition known as SCID (Severe Combined Immunodeficiency) He has a defective immune system and the only cure is a bone marrow transplant. The cost is very high, approximately GBP100,000, equivalent to about USD150,000. Without a transplant, a SCID baby rarely sees his first birthday.

Please help him live. A contribution from you, however small, can give us life. We thank you for reading this mail. Please pass this to your friends. Bank details follow:

We were waiting for our baby's passport to arrive. We were making our travel arrangements and were in the process of booking flights. My company, while helpful, wanted confirmation about when I would start work over there. Their office wasn't in London but in Luton, thirty minutes away, so my husband would have to be in the hospital while I stayed close to work for most of the week. This kind of detail made me impatient when there were so many more important issues to think about. I worried that we might not even be allowed into the country with such an ill baby. We needed documentation from Great Ormond Street Hospital confirming treatment. We needed to have available cash. The hospital needed us to transfer a deposit. We needed letters from my company confirming they would process my work permit and provide proof of my salary slips.

Now, when I think back to those days with so many big and small things to plan, it was like a giant mosaic, like dominoes in a stack. I'm amazed and astonished that I dared to dream it could be possible. That our baby could leave India for expensive medical treatment in the UK. So tied up was I with phone calls and emails, I managed to overlook, or maybe ignore, one very simple thing.

How well was our baby?

There were no warning signs that his condition was getting

worse. He was on strong medication; antibiotics, antiviral drugs and prophylactics. Bottles and pills were piled on the table next to our bed. There was nothing to give me cause for concern about how he would cope on a long flight and we'd planned to give him painkillers and Calpol before we boarded. We carried on planning incessantly, frantically.

22nd June 2000 is the date that remains on play. Forever. The day my husband and I were both called at work. We raced through the city's traffic to our flat where more cheques had arrived through the letter box. Our baby's passport had been delivered, it's issue date 22nd June 2000.

But he would never need a visa for the UK.

The date on his passport marked the date of his entry into another world.

The great well of adrenalin that had pulled me through the past frenetic, stressful weeks deflated like a limp balloon. I held my cold, stiff little baby in my arms. Then outrage at the unjustness of it all burned alongside a sorrow too deep for words.

13

After the funeral, which was no more than a hasty burial, after everyone, including Suchitra, had left, my husband, mother-in-law and I sat in the living room in silence, unsure what to do next. There were no emails to send, no travel arrangements to make, no packing to do. My husband asked if I wanted to go out for dinner. It seemed almost a sensible thing to do, go to one of our favourite restaurants called Peter Cat in Park Street and order Chello Kebab like we often did. After all, our evening was empty. It also seemed like a ridiculous thing to do. Your world has just collapsed and you decide to go out for a meal! I agreed since there didn't seem any reason not to. There was no baby to look after. However, just the thought of walking downstairs, getting into the car, driving to a busy restaurant and ordering food filled me with utter exhaustion.

'I can't go out.'

'What do we eat then?'

'Suchitra hasn't cooked anything,' my mother-in-law said.

'I don't know. Something. Anything. Nothing.'

I don't remember what we did eat that evening, but I know that I didn't want to talk to anyone. Instead I went back to my laptop and wrote to my SCID group. Long emails of love, wishes, virtual hugs and philosophical messages arrived all through the night. Hearing back from families who had stared at death or were staring at unwell children every day, made me feel less alone.

My parents asked us to come and stay with them for a while to get away from the flat and to rest and recuperate. I insisted I was fine and could cope. Nothing could comfort me. I slept for hours and still felt tired. Later, I would read that extreme tiredness often accompanied grief. A couple of days later, my despair was so overwhelming that my husband booked flights to Chennai, and made plans to stay with my parents and sister's family.

We drove to Pondicherry, a coastal town, French territory until 1954. I had never been there before, though I had always wanted to. The influence of the French still remained in the wide boulevards, the names of the streets, French words intersecting with Tamil ones. We stayed in a hotel by the sea. In the morning, I woke and looked at the waves crashing on the shores, people doing yoga on the green lawns. Serenity. I could sense it, almost reach out and touch it but I was in too much turmoil to soak it up. Nothing felt enough. Nothing helped.

My parents took me to the ashram, to the samadhi[7] of The Mother and Sri Aurobindo. A feeling of calm swept over you as soon as you entered the gates to the cottage and left behind the crowds and heat of the main roads. You had to remain completely silent once at the actual samadhi, a large rectangular black slab of marble, decorated with fresh flowers – bright marigolds, red roses, fragrant white jasmine arranged in circles and ovals. In the centre, a dozen incense sticks burned. People sat silent and meditated or walked in reverence. I felt sorrow, deep anger and frustration that nothing could save my son, that this country I was born in could do nothing for me. I felt suffocated amidst

---

7 Samadhi: burial place, a shrine especially of saints

the peace and beauty. I walked around the path as directed, then waited for my parents outside.

'After my son died, I felt the same. I threw away all the idols I possessed and stopped praying to The Mother for years,' my mother said, when she joined me. 'There is no point being angry with God though. Give in, pray to God that you will have a healthy child next time.'

'If not God, then who is to blame?' I asked.

'No one is to blame. This is the way of the universe.'

I was in no mood to listen to philosophy. I felt I would be disloyal to my baby if I stopped grieving.

In the evening, they took me shopping as a distraction. I loved handicrafts and jewellery. I looked at beautiful earrings but there was no eagerness in my fingers as I picked one up.

'Do you like that one? Or maybe this one here, isn't it pretty?' my mother said.

'Yes, they are nice. All nice…but let's go back. I am tired.'

'Don't you want to buy anything? Or do you want to go somewhere else? They have a great shop just on the other side of the road,' my father said.

I had already walked out. They followed. They were waiting for me to ask eagerly for something, to demand, 'Yes I want this!' I understood they wanted to give me something, anything, to compensate for my pain but I wanted nothing. My father walked ahead, worry lines on his forehead. My mother looked around for another shop that might interest me.

'Time will heal,' people said. 'Forget this and have another child. It will all be well. It will never happen again.'

But what if it does happen again? For future pregnancies,

there was a one in four chance the dice would roll with the same outcome, that I would have another boy with the same fatal condition and my story would have the same ending. In my support group, there was one family with four children all of whom had SCID. Another family had two daughters who were carriers who each had two sons with X-SCID. But these children were having treatment and so far were well because they lived in America.

14

We had heard about the boy who had been born before. We heard it discussed in whispers. We knew about *that boy* who came and went too quickly. My parents' marriage was arranged when both were really young but this was fairly usual then in small town India. My father was a doctor, and my mother a student of English literature, very much into music and poetry. Their baby boy was born healthy but by the time he was three months old he became more and more unwell, again and again. During those periods, his mouth was covered with thrush and he was in too much pain to swallow food. He had diarrhoea and was getting weaker every day. The doctors couldn't work out what was wrong and were unable to treat him. He died when he was six months old after countless doctor visits, countless courses of medicine, a mere shadow of the healthy beautiful boy he had been at birth. If only my parents hadn't been living in a small town, without adequate medical care, if only the doctors had been better. My mother harboured these regrets for years. It was especially poignant for the entire community because he was the first born and a boy. Boys were desired and longed for. Everyone lamented with my parents. They were in shock, not knowing why their baby had died, not knowing what had gone wrong.

After the death of their son, born ironically on the day of

their wedding anniversary, my mother had prayed for daughters. Her prayers were answered because a year later she had a girl, my sister. Three years later she had me – although others hoped that I would be a boy. My mother held fast to her prayers and her wish to be blessed with two girls, never mind if the whole community thought they needed a son. She wanted to dress her two daughters in the same clothes like dolls, and raise them to be as strong as trees, as self-sufficient as men.

Ironically, even with both daughters grown up with professional careers – my sister a doctor and me an engineer with an MBA – friends of my parents continued to commiserate with them. 'Only two girls? No sons?'

After I lost my baby, I thought of him often, the one who had come before. Strange to think that I might have had a brother.

As kids, if we fought, I would say to my sister teasingly, 'I wish our brother was here. He would not be as horrid as you.'

'And if he had been here, you wouldn't be!' she once retorted.

It was true of course. Had he survived, my parents would not have had another child.

I cried now for my baby, and for the baby who came before, my brother who died after repeated illnesses simply because no one could give him a diagnosis. I thought about my parents, my father a young doctor himself, running from one colleague to the other, asking the most senior doctors to come and take a look at his first born, begging everyone to help him. I thought about my young, beautiful mother, helplessly wondering why her baby wasn't recovering. Her father, my grandfather, was a renowned doctor and even he did not understand what was wrong. His helplessness was now being mirrored in my own father. It was life repeating itself in a circle.

Except now we finally knew what was wrong.

But even if they had known, my parents would not have been able to do anything. If we had no options for treatment in India in the year 2000, what chance did they have in 1968? Years later, even as recently as 2018, Indian parents who joined the SCID group would still be asking the same questions. Where can we go? What do we do? How do we raise the money to treat our child abroad? Inevitably, their babies had been injected with the BCG vaccine since this was a routine vaccine in India, and this live vaccine would have created havoc in their little bodies. I would hear of parents losing not one, but two babies, and still hoping that next time the story of genetics would be different. The dice would be cast in favour of a healthy baby.

'Just pray for a girl next time,' my mother said. 'Then everything will be well.'

I didn't believe that my prayers would be heard. I didn't believe I could expect God to protect us when we hadn't even tried to change our own situation. I had prayed for a healthy baby but my prayer wasn't heard. Why would it be heard next time?

Many years later, I would read that the Gita says that one must always act with viveka[8] to develop an intelligence born of determination. Only then would Grace act to help you.

---

8 Viveka: A Sanskrit term translated into English as discernment.

15

After staying a few days in Chennai and Pondicherry, we went to a resort in the hills of Karnataka. We wore the mask of a normal family on holiday. Everyone was trying to convince me that I still had a lot to live for. In the hills I walked alone, and thought, what if I jumped down from here, from this peak, what if I just let go? They were keeping an eye on me, and I could do nothing of the sort.

'We are your own. We have been with you for so many years. Don't we mean anything to you?' my parents asked.

I was lucky to have a loving family but didn't want to share my loneliness with anyone. It was mine, all mine.

Then it was time to go back to Calcutta. Stepping into the empty flat in Calcutta was one of the hardest things I have ever done. Suchitra had cleared the rooms including all the things belonging to our baby, as if he hadn't ever been there. You can remove all traces of a person from a house, but not your heart or your arms. The night before he died, he couldn't even breast feed. On medical advice I had tried to continue because it was one way to pass on some of my immunity but his neck was so stiff that he couldn't turn his face. Perhaps his spine was affected by TB. We would never know. The table near the bed was now empty, the menagerie of medicines disposed of.

Our neighbours watched in silence when we came back. Our sorrow numbed them as well.

In the office, people welcomed me back but most avoided the obvious topic. One young, unmarried colleague asked, 'Did you cry a lot?' I had no answer. Others said, 'I could never cope with such pain,' as if one had a choice. I quickly understood that some people couldn't comprehend the magnitude of the loss of a child. Work was my only saving grace and throwing myself back into the game of sales and numbers was, in some strange way, redeeming.

We tried to piece our life back together. We decided to take up swimming classes but we hardly cared if we sank or floated. We often went out for dinner in a restaurant where we watched Calcutta from the top floor. There were people everywhere, families, children, everyone had children. Everyone seemed so noisy. I would come back feeling exhausted. Crowded places tired me so quickly. Calcutta would remain forever a gloomy, dismal city for me.

The housekeeper had thankfully left before our baby passed away so Suchitra did the cooking, ironing and cleaning. There was a strong bond with her and I couldn't ask her not to come. She faced the empty mornings, saw the bathtub she would no longer bathe him in, the pans and plates she would no longer use for his meals, the bed in which she would never lay him. I could escape. I went to work, I travelled, I planned milestones. Still a part of the SCID group, I was now part of their stories, part of a family in which children fell ill and recovered. That virtual world brought me messages of hope, love and warmth and I preferred it to the real one.

Supported by the group, I planned to get myself tested to

confirm the X-SCID carrier status. The National Institute of Health (NIH) in America offered free testing to support their ongoing research. I wrote to them and within the day had their reply. They had a collaboration with a medical courier in Delhi who would come to our house and collect blood samples, all at the NIH's expense. As well as samples from me, they asked if any of our baby's DNA had been retained. Then they would be able to isolate the exact point in the chromosomes where the defect occurred. I wrote to Dr. Verghese expecting a negative reply, but his response was quick. Anticipating the outcome, they had kept samples of his DNA. I never asked what they had stored. Had they extracted the DNA from his blood or skin or hair? Which part of him was still living, still telling his story?

Someone came to our flat to take blood samples. I sat at the dining table while they filled vial after vial. The challenge for the courier was to get the blood from Calcutta to Bethesda in the heart of America in forty-eight hours, but they managed it with some clever logistics.

Within days, a report was emailed to me. It confirmed that our baby had X-SCID and I was a carrier. It went a step further to specify the exact mutation in my IL2RG gene that created this anomaly. Over the years I would read it often, to tell myself it was ordained, it was all in the genes. There was nothing I could have done.

The NIH was happy to test others in the family – my mother, sister, aunts, cousins and any women of childbearing age. All they wanted in return was our details for their X-SCID database. My sister already had a healthy son but there was a chance that she had passed on the lucky X and that a future pregnancy would carry a risk. She agreed to be tested. The results came back confirming she wasn't a carrier.

My maternal grandmother had four daughters and three sons. All her sons – my uncles – were well. However, my mother's elder sister, my aunt, now spoke of a boy who had been born to my grandmother and had died in days, his mouth covered with thrush. This was years before she was born, and she had a vague memory of being told this story when she was a child. None of the other siblings including my mother could validate it. My grandparents had died long before so there was no way to confirm if this was true. Had there been a baby boy before the daughters? And if there was, had he died from poor medical care, so common in the 1930s, or was he also born with X-SCID? If he was born with X-SCID, and my grandmother was a carrier, was she simply incredibly lucky to have three healthy sons in a row? My mother's other sisters, my aunts, all had healthy boys. So if my grandmother was a carrier, either she had passed on the defective X only to my mother, or else the other daughters did have a faulty X but had been fortunate enough to have healthy sons. That was a lot of luck! The only way to end the speculation was to have everyone tested and the NIH was eager to comply. However, my aunts lived in small towns without international access, and to get bloods from there to Bethseda in the stipulated forty-eight hours was close to impossible. More importantly, apart from my mother, no one seemed interested. SCID sounded esoteric so my cousins believed such a thing would never happen to them, and they were right, it never did. Everyone, without exception, went on to produce healthy boys. Surely it couldn't be luck, with me the only unlucky one, or could it? The only other explanation was that the mutation had happened in my mother who passed it on to me. It was entirely possible, the doctors said.

We would never know.

I was trying to fill my time and my restless mind but nothing I did felt enough. One day, while reading emails from my SCID family, I decided that I would like to be near children who were unwell. SCID was unknown in India but there were plenty of organisations working for cancer. I went to meet the *Make a Wish* foundation, a worldwide organisation which worked to fulfil the last wish of terminally ill children. In Calcutta, it was run by a young man who was a leukaemia survivor. Though recovered, the fight with cancer had left him frail and wasted. I sat in the deep upholstered chair in his office and told him my story and why I wanted to work with them. They needed volunteers, they needed donations, however small. I agreed to both. I told them my story. I spoke to them of my grief and how I felt I had to do something to keep me going. They kept my details. Perhaps they were a little too moved by my grief because I never heard back.

I was always an avid reader of fiction, but now I read only about death, life after death, the causes of death in infancy. I asked where do souls go? *The Tibetan Book of Living and Dying* was my Bible which I tried to understand as well as I could. I read a memoir written by a mother whose only daughter and granddaughter died after eating poisonous mushrooms in the hills of India. I wrote to the author sharing my story, and she replied, acknowledging my grief and my appreciation of her moving book. She said writers needed sensitive readers and thanked me for being one. By acknowledging the grief in other people's lives, I tried to make sense of mine. I tried to understand why sorrow hits only some of us. But at times, I was also angry about the injustice of it happening to me. Why couldn't God listen to my prayer to save my child? I had never been very religious before, but now I stopped praying. Not for me a God who hadn't listened.

Though God hadn't listened, man had. Our balm was the empathy, support and help we received from others.

16

If previously I had felt Calcutta carried an air of depression with its never-ending tracts of poverty, now it became a crescendo of panic. The anger and helplessness threatened to choke me. Nothing could comfort me. Every day I had to look for a reason to get out of bed.

Have you held a baby, dead, in your arms? Do you know how suddenly, in just a few minutes, the soft dimpled limbs become dimensionless and rigid? The breath is sucked out and a woodenness nests in the body. What does lifeless truly mean, do you know? The empty flat mocked me, voices called out, rarely soothing, always admonishing: What a mother! You passed on your defective genes! You live in a place where you couldn't save your child, and not only that, you weren't even there to say goodbye! You were at work. What a mother!!!

The world felt hollow. Everyone wanted to comfort and soothe me but their own lives called them back. They carried on with their routines and their happiness, leaving us outside, on the brink.

I couldn't follow him but I had to escape these voices. I would have to move somewhere else where there was hope. Where I could slowly rebuild myself. Where I could heal in little portions.

I had to leave this city, this country. I had to get away from the heat to somewhere cool and green.

The only way I could escape to another place was with a new job. The initiative of transferring to the England office, started as a quest to save my baby, had stalled. It was an expense and commitment which the company now saw no reason for, considering they could hire sales people locally. Due to some internal restructuring, I was in the Asia Pacific sales team, reporting to an Australian boss in the Sydney office. A father of three little kids, he had been quick to commiserate. 'My heart is with you,' he had written when the news of my baby's death was announced in the office. He promised he would try to move me to Hong Kong or maybe Thailand where he planned to set up office. They were not transplant centres for SCID, I thought, but at least I could escape from Calcutta. Then I heard of some new openings in America. They wanted business consultants and while I was more into sales and marketing, the CEO in the American head office thought I could have a go. He had been gutted that he – they – could do nothing for me when we had to watch our baby die. I needed to convince the management in Calcutta that I would be suitable for this position, but they didn't buy my reasons of wanting a new challenge and wanting to move on from direct sales roles. They knew my story too well. They knew that the drive behind my application for the job was to leave the country. They said I wouldn't be a good fit.

The place I really wanted to go to, the place I was sure would be conducive to both of us, the place I fell in love with a little bit more every time I travelled there, was England. I yearned to go to London, to stand in front of Great Ormond Street Hospital, even though my baby hadn't made it. That became my dream and obsession. I hated everything around me more and more and every day drove me further into despair.

'You are not yourself anymore. I wish I could do something to help you,' my friend in England said. He had been helping me with the fund collection.

'Find me a job. I want to get out of here,' I said, not expecting he could actually help.

'I know a great recruitment agent. Chris will find you something, I'm sure.'

I wasn't convinced. I was a Telecoms Engineer but had never worked in a technical role. Software jobs were the easiest ones to transfer abroad but I was a salesperson, an MBA who was trained in the business practices of a certain country. Why would they want me with no specific expertise?

Chris, an enthusiastic, young guy, called me soon after. He told me my experience was brilliant, my education was brilliant, in short, everything about me was exactly what organisations needed. I tried to feel as confident as he sounded.

Within a few days he had arranged some interviews for me. Under the guise of a handover before moving to a different region, I went to London. I had five interviews over two days. When the interviewers asked me why I wanted to move to England, I replied that I was an ambitious sales person and needed more challenges. The Telecommunications market was much more advanced in Europe. I wanted my career to flourish. They liked the answer. Employers like to see drive and ambition, whether fuelled by despair or not. The mother in me tucked herself into layers of sorrow and stayed silent, giving way to the doer in me, the promiser of dreams.

One of the organisations, an international Telecoms company

made me an offer. They agreed to process my work permit, a process which could take up to a couple of months or more. Around that time, I was called for an interview at a reputed Indian company in Bangalore. The interviewer asked me about my family and I ended up telling him about the death of my baby. He was moved. 'How could you have done so much? Met all your sales targets, had a baby, and been through all this?' I could only smile and say thank you. I hadn't thought my efforts were commendable in any way. I was burning with a huge sense of failure and guilt. Even though I knew it was not my fault, I couldn't forgive myself that I lived well while my genes created havoc in my baby. The medical system in my country let him down and we could do nothing to save him. This stranger's sudden praise was heart-warming.

They made me an attractive offer. The temptation was strong to give up my dream of moving to Britain and to stay close to family. Moving out of Calcutta to Bangalore would give us the longed for change of environment and my husband could ask for a transfer in his company. It would be easy and comfortable. But what about the future? What if the dice rolled again the same way as it had before? No one could help us.

My work permit arrived in my Calcutta flat a couple of days later. Sitting on the same bed where my baby had lain some months back, I stared at the coloured piece of paper in my hands, not believing this could have happened. A work permit for the maximum possible time of five years. A job in London. I remember holding on to the sides of the bed, tears streaming down my face. I knew what I wanted to do. I knew exactly what I had to do.

I politely refused the Bangalore offer.

Because it had taken them months to organise my work permit, the UK company was becoming impatient and wanted me to start work sooner rather than later so we agreed a date four weeks ahead. That gave us very little time to get ready.

We planned the packing up of our home. We gave our possessions to friends and family including the beautiful things we had bought from fairs and auctions – the hand carved wooden chairs, the embroidered rug, the terracotta sculpture. We gave away the car we had bought with our savings. I valued none of it. It didn't matter.

I was excited and relieved at the thought of leaving but I couldn't bring myself to share the news with Suchitra because she would be the one facing the repercussions and she would be the one having to look for a new job. We would pay her several months salary but there was little more we could do. I procrastinated for several days and said nothing but she sensed something was different and asked if we were going to leave. I told her about my new job in London and she asked why we weren't thinking of having another baby. Our babushuna will come back, she said. I knew and often heard this belief that a dead child would return reincarnated as another baby if conception was soon after the first child's death. I didn't believe it. I told her I couldn't continue to live in that flat or the city and even perhaps the country any longer. I had to go, the further the better.

A couple of weeks later, in our flat now empty of all our possessions, we said goodbye to Suchitra, I broke down on her shoulder, the same shoulder our baby had loved and snuggled into, and wept.

My husband and I flew to London.

SECTION 3 – BLOCKAGE – ANGER

1

We arrived in London on a cold spring day in March 2001. We stayed for some days with a family friend, then in a hotel until we found a flat to rent.

My office was centrally located, near Trafalgar Square, so we had no geographical constraints. We could go north, south, east or west. I pored over maps and traced the names of streets, such interesting quaint names, and we took the tube and travelled across the city. I remember the snow in March. It came on suddenly, soft white flakes all around us one day when we walked outside. It took a while to register that it was snow and even the locals seemed taken aback that it had arrived in late spring. Over the following years, the unpredictability of the weather would continue to make me smile.

I never imagined that a place could be a balm, could soothe and nourish, could make me want to live again, even free me. London was all that for me. Being in the city, walking her roads, strolling along the river and looking in shops along the Strand – it was like a baptism. As if the city was trying to welcome and woo me. As if it was the city's responsibility to help me forget, to help me heal.

As a child, people used to say that I was always lost in my own world, nose buried in books.

'Is she aware that there is a world outside those books?' my mother often said in desperation.

'She doesn't even know what's on her plate and what she's eating!' exasperated relatives observed, since I was often reading at the dinner table

Here in London, that world of books came alive. At every turn of the street, there was a landmark or a sign to take me to my make-believe world. The names of the streets, the blue plaques, characters from Dickens or Harry Potter were right here in the streets I walked. And in the crowd, where every face was different, it didn't matter where I was from. What did colour or caste or creed matter. Here in this melting pot, I could forget who I was and what had happened to me. I could pretend to be the person I appeared to be just another young girl, just one half of another couple in a marvellous city out enjoying themselves. No one knew our story.

Several of my colleagues were the same age or a couple of years younger than me, still not married, still no kids. Others, perhaps ten years older, were mostly settled with families. My colleagues accepted me as one of them. They knew I had married quite young, but perhaps they expected that as part of my culture.

I heard their stories. So many stories, so many women. There was a beautiful European woman who, over soup at lunch, told me about her miscarriages, one after the other, and how she was desperately trying to conceive and keep. My story shocked her but made her feel that she wasn't alone since others had known worse loss. There was a woman who was waiting for her boyfriend to propose because she wanted to have two children before she was thirty-five. There was a woman who when I asked, 'What would you like to be in the next five years?', replied, 'Fat and pregnant.' I wanted to tell them all I had been there already. I wanted to say that there was a lot more to life and that babies came with pain. I couldn't believe that these women, so independent, so confident, were trying so hard to have the very thing I was trying to run away from. One of my friends was having her second baby.

'But why?' I asked.

They found my question hilarious.

Those who heard my story commiserated with me, and then asked the inevitable question. 'Would you have another one? When?'

My answer varied.

In practical terms, I was in a vulnerable position. I had a work permit sponsored by the company. Though I was happy working with them, they were cutting staff because of the economic situation so I was not in a secure position. My husband was offered a job in London and was taken on without a work permit which saved him a lot of paperwork. So I had to hang on to my job and my work permit. It was hardly the time to think of having a baby and going on maternity leave.

Apart from that, I knew there were several hoops I would need to jump through. Dr. Verghese had told me in Vellore that if I ever got pregnant again, I needed to contact him at fourteen to sixteen weeks so they could do a prenatal diagnostic test, either a Chorionic Villi sampling (CVS) or an amniocentesis. These were invasive tests and involved a needle being inserted into the foetus for a sample to check if it was a boy or girl. If it was a girl, I could relax because the worst case scenario was that she would be a carrier like me and my mother. If we were in India, there would be no test for SCID so if I was carrying a boy, they would suggest a termination. If we were in London, they *could* test for SCID and we could make the decision to terminate or choose to go ahead knowing treatment was available. I knew enough children who were living normal lives after bone marrow transplants.

Being in London made a lot more sense.

I had all the facts but no plans yet to act on them.

2

Two years passed, living in and loving London.

On my birthday, I was in Barcelona for a work conference and in the evening, we had a customer event where we all went for dinner to a quaint restaurant in the Ramblas. My colleague had ordered a cake and as everyone sang Happy Birthday, someone said, 'Let's give her birthday bumps!' So, there I was, thrown up in the air by colleagues and customers. Great laughter and joy with me feeling weightless in their arms, and as young as I did in university. Briefly!

They say that grief is like a little stone in your shoe. You don't always feel it but you know it's there, ever-present and, from time to time, it bites into your soul to remind you that all isn't well. I felt that sharp pain sometimes, out of the blue, unbidden. Sitting in the tube and noticing a baby asleep in his mother's arms, I felt his weight and sensed his plump fingers on hers, the tired mother holding firmly on to her child, shifting her arms so the baby slept comfortably when the train lurched. It reminded me of what had been, how a baby reaches out and grabs the mother's hair, how a baby's fingers touch the mother's face with trust and confidence, knowing that she will never be unkind. The emptiness I felt was tangible, a physical sensation of wanting, of longing, of wishing I could have my baby back. In the middle of Covent Garden, hearing Eric Clapton's *Would you know my name if I saw you in heaven*? my tears flowed as I felt his pain. Years later, I would read about the tragic circumstances of his son's death when he fell from their high rise apartment in New York, and once again, the tears would fall for a family I didn't know, and it didn't matter if it was my baby or this little boy who died, the very loss of a child for anyone was so upsetting. Over the years, people would comment on how strong I was and how well I was handling it all. Yet I would find myself weeping watching a Disney movie, like when Tarzan's parents died and he was found by the gorillas. I wept for the baby and both the mothers while chiding myself for being silly. It's only an animated film! Does it warrant so many tears?

I read a lot; philosophy, religion, self-help, memoirs. My friend from the SCID group often said, 'Let go and let God.' I felt that leaving things to God meant anything could happen! I rejected a passive, unquestioning faith but I believed in doing your own best and accepting the outcome.

After two years in the UK, we bought a house, a suitable semi with a garden in the suburbs, not even picking up all the nudges from the seller to the estate agent to friends and colleagues. 'Just the right thing to do before starting a family. Move out of the city, move into a place with a garden.' For us, the decision was purely economical and a need for more space yet perhaps subconsciously we were planning a particular future.

Soon after moving, I registered with the local GP. The surgery was at the end of our road, a mere five-minute walk. Finally, I asked for an appointment. Finally, I was ready to talk.

3

It seemed anything but a surgery, a detached house with the name of the medical practice in blue on the front door. The receptionist asked me to take a seat along with the others, mostly older people or mothers with young babies. Magazines were strewn on the table, a good mix of Elle, Cosmopolitan, House and Garden. It wasn't intimidating – Noddy could have been sitting next to me – and I started to relax.

I had been waiting for more than fifteen minutes when a woman came out to call me in. I followed her into a room and only when she took her seat did I realise she was the doctor. This was one of the first differences I noticed in the medical systems in India and the UK. Back in India, an assistant or lackey would call a patient in, not the doctors themselves.

I blurted, 'You are so young!'

Dr. Patel, a pleasant, young, British Asian, smiled. Unknown to me, this was a face I would meet many times over the next few years. It was easy to talk to her. I didn't know whether I was blabbering or speaking sense, but she got the gist. She drew the familiar XX and XY diagram to explain X-SCID once again. It never failed to fascinate me, the small twist of fate which could mean life or death, the passing of a genetic code from the parents to child. She agreed it was good for us to be prepared, even though we had no plans yet to try again for a baby. She would refer me to the genetics department in Guy's and St. Thomas' in London.

After a few months the appointment at Guy's was confirmed. The hospital is beside London Bridge station, an easy journey from home. As I sat in the waiting room, reading the stories about the miracles this genetics team routinely carried out, I was humbled and grateful that I could be here, in this room, with a right to be here. Like I did almost every day, I thanked my stars that someone had written these years in London in my fate.

The team of doctors I met were at the forefront of medical research, yet so down to earth, so polite. Once again, they explained the primary immune deficiencies. Once again they spelled out the options available to us

The first option was to do nothing. Conceive naturally and hope for the best, and test the baby's blood count at birth. A very low white blood cell count was an indicator of SCID. If the baby was affected, then the treatment was a bone marrow transplant which would be carried out in Great Ormond Street hospital. I knew of children in my support group who'd had transplants and were living normal lives. This was a viable option, as long as you lived in a place where the treatment was available and if you knew your child was affected at, or before, birth.

The second option was to conceive naturally and around twelve weeks opt for a pre-natal diagnostic test – either the CVS[9] at 12-14 weeks or amniocentesis at around 16 weeks. Both tests have pros and cons. The CVS carries a higher risk of miscarriage but because it's carried out relatively early in the pregnancy, a termination, if necessary, is an option. The amniocentesis carries

---

9   CVS: Chorionic Villus Sampling, an invasive procedure to obtain a sample from the foetus for further tests

a lower risk of miscarriage because it's done later. Both tests reveal the child's gender and if it's a boy, chromosomes are isolated to check for SCID. If our baby tested positive, we could decide on a termination or I could carry the baby to term and he would be enrolled for treatment.

The third option was to eliminate all risk of a defective X chromosome by genetically selecting the gender of the baby by a process called pre-implementation genetic diagnosis, PGD, very like in-vitro fertilisation, IVF, except that after the embryos are harvested only a female embryo is inserted into the womb. Male embryos are discarded because it's impossible to diagnose at the chromosomal level. There is no way we would have a boy if we took the route of a PGD.

'Not that we want to,' I smiled in answer. 'We both always wanted a girl.'

Unfortunately, it wasn't straightforward. The success rate was rather low because while the process was similar to IVF, there was the additional complication of all male embryos being discarded.

The doctor herself had opted for CVS because she had been over forty when she conceived. She described the procedure as mildly uncomfortable but not painful. Of the three options discussed, the team seemed to be leaning towards the second. We too felt this was the most practical solution. I was apprehensive of needles and drugs and other paraphernalia so wasn't keen on in-vitro fertilisation.

I decided to do some research so that I was prepared with all the information I could find before I tried to get pregnant. I signed up on Netmums and joined a message board about invasive tests. I again sent emails to complete strangers, introducing myself and telling them my story of loss. Strangers, most of whom I would never meet, replied with poignant emails of love. They wrote too about their own experiences and the tests they had undergone. For many, the pain of the invasive test was the least of the problems. For many, the worst was knowing that they carried a child with a serious condition for which there was no cure which brought with it the impossible choice of deciding to terminate or keeping a baby who had an uncertain, possibly difficult future. I made friends with a woman who had been through this. She had CVS after abnormalities were picked up in a routine scan that suggested the baby could have a problem with the diaphragm. The couple didn't terminate since she had conceived after repeated miscarriages and had no intention of giving up. Her baby girl died, a day old, in her mother's arms. Her stomach and lungs were fused, like the doctors had predicted. Not once did she regret the pregnancy. She said that giving up on her daughter was never an option. We sensed we were kindred spirits and months and years later, often emailed each other. Over the years, I would often turn to her, when I needed support, instead of friends I had grown up with.

My husband and I debated whether we could terminate a pregnancy if we were told that the baby tested positive for SCID. Having lost one child, could we take the decision to kill an embryo?

'SCID is fully curable,' I kept repeating. 'Here in London.'

'If it is curable, why have a test which carries a risk of miscarriage?' My husband kept asking.

'Well it *is* curable, but it's a very complex condition and the treatment has side effects. Why not simplify things and not go through a transplant?' A bone marrow transplant normally involves chemotherapy which also has side effects. Though we knew Dr. Radley from Duke University in America follows a gentler protocol where she doesn't administer chemotherapy. But there's a serious downside. In many cases, the immune system doesn't reconstitute itself. Most of her patients need to have lifelong infusions of immunoglobulins.

Was it fair to put a tiny baby through so much invasive treatment? Wasn't it better to opt for genetic testing and have a girl? Or was it better to try naturally and have a test during the pregnancy? Surely, surely, it wouldn't happen a second time? So it could be a girl or an unaffected boy. The dice *could* roll in our favour. Why were we forgetting that?

So we thought. So we reasoned. I had by now lost touch with my SCID support group as my old email account had been closed from lack of use. My friends were now other mums and mums-to-be on Netmums and I discussed the options with them too.

I spent hours going over something I thought I would surely face one day. I had no idea that an invasive test or the lack of one was never to be my problem.

4

Life and London had me in their grip. The freedom I felt in those years was the manna I craved. We decorated our house, we went on holidays, we invited friends home, mostly couples like us who had moved from India, not after a saga, but due to a job and economic conditions. Some were old friends from Calcutta days who knew the past but didn't ask me about it. Sometimes new friends would ask why we didn't have children – after so many years of marriage – and depending on their emotional intelligence, I would choose to tell them or not.

My company continued to have redundancies. We all worried about when it would be our turn and everyone was concerned for me because I was one of the most vulnerable. If I didn't have a job, I would have to leave the UK, literally the next day. One day, an ex-colleague from the Calcutta company met me. His company was trying to rebuild a team and they remembered me and my success. Would I like to go back to them and give it a try? Could I weave my magic for them again? The company would sponsor my work permit and offer me a role with a higher salary.

It made sense to move, even though my travelling would involve regions outside Europe. Once again, the company seemed to bring me luck because within a year I had closed new business deals and met all my targets. One more year and we could be permanent UK residents. This would mean that the pressure about work permits would end.

It was almost four years after moving to London that we finally decided to try for another baby. I tried to push the old and new fears aside and concentrate on one thing – to have a girl. If you pray and believe, miracles will happen. God is kind. God will help. You need to be positive. You need to believe. Above all, there was a strong assurance from my family and almost anyone who knew our story that it couldn't happen again.

My mother said, 'I had two girls after my boy. I forgot all the sorrow when you were born. So will you. You will have a little girl.'

All will be well.

I expected that just like last time, I wouldn't have to wait long. I started planning my world trips to fit in with my possible pregnancy. Could I attend the GSM conference in Cape Town this year in November? If I conceived next month, I would be about six months pregnant so that wouldn't be a good time. However, if I conceived later than that, I would still be able to take a long flight.

We planned to hire a nanny. We didn't want to send our baby to daycare and, more importantly, my travelling meant we needed a carer who could offer flexibility. My thoughts and plans were racing ahead, once again believing I was in control of my life once again, forgetting that plans and worries don't always come to fruition.

5

Unlike last time, nothing happened the first month. Nothing happened the second month either or for months after. Each month passed with no good news or titters of excitement. I wrote to other mums on Netmums. 'Take heart,' they advised. 'It's only been six months and sometimes it can take up to a year. You have to give yourself time before worrying.' And because I was travelling so much, maybe I was missing the dates for conception.

I educated myself on the science of ovulation. For someone who had never been tuned to monthly cycles or troubled by aches and pains at that time of the month, I now had to listen to my body which apparently was giving me signals. If I listened, I would know when I was at my most fertile. My friend from Netmums who was trying to get pregnant after several miscarriages, explained how to watch out for the smaller clues like changes in the vaginal discharge. These were personal details I needed to monitor so that I would know the perfect moment for conception.

And if I didn't want to rely on my instincts, there were ovulation sticks to help predict when I was at my most fertile. An ovulation kit came optimistically with a pregnancy test. It was rather expensive, but it was a one off, and, very soon I would be needing the pregnancy test too, I thought.

Nothing. Yet another month, yet another hurried check in the office bathroom and utter disbelief at failure. Then the gradual build-up of worry – was something wrong? Why wasn't it happening? The second time is so much easier, I had heard other women say.

I had to go back for those ovulation packs.

By now, all my friends had more news. I was getting used to the three magic words, 'I am pregnant,' which a friend would announce with a blush at a lunch or dinner while declining a proffered glass of wine which I accepted and downed with alacrity. Sometimes I had to rush to the bathroom to hide my tears. Make-up helped. I would talk about my job, my travels around the world, my activities, a trip to Namibia, a wine tasting event in La Defense Grande Arche, my aerobics classes, my gym regime – things pregnant women couldn't do.

No one knew that we were trying and the more I heard the delight of others with good news, the more I painted a picture of myself as the busy career woman, so engrossed in her own life that she couldn't be bothered with babies. My hangers hung with fashionable clothes and my drawers were lined with shoes – the outer veneer of a successful life. I acted nonchalant.

6

After almost nine months of trying to get pregnant, I went to the GP. This time I didn't have an appointment with my usual Dr. Patel but another doctor who was equally sympathetic. My story was in their records and I was always met with kindness. I told the doctor how quickly I'd conceived last time and was slightly concerned that second time round it was taking longer. I expected her to assuage my fears and tell me not to worry. Just a matter of time and nine months is nothing. The fact of nine months wasn't lost on me. I could have given birth by now. Instead I saw her write in her notes, *'nine months of trying.'*

'There is something called secondary infertility when you have successfully conceived once but develop problems later. Don't worry, we can find out if something is wrong. The best way is to test the man first because it's a simpler test. Once that's ruled out, we test the woman.'

'And what tests would those be?'

'Scans, blood tests, there are a few.'

We were visiting family in India in a couple of weeks. The doctor suggested my husband come immediately, this week, so we'd have the results before we left. My tests could be done when we were back.

'Don't worry. Everything may be fine, just a matter of time,' she assured me as I stood up to leave.

I was sure it would be fine. It was worry and the stress of modern life, that's all. I was commuting for three hours every day; taking a train and then the tube to get to work. I had to achieve my annual sales targets and was travelling to far-flung locations in Africa to meet prospective clients. I was worrying about acronyms galore, CVS, SCID and so on. Surely these were reasons enough for the delay in conceiving.

My husband's test came back normal. The onus was on me.

The two-week holiday in India flew past meeting friends and family. I went to Chennai to visit my sister for a couple of days before flying back to London. As a doctor herself, she made a suggestion. 'Why don't you come with me to the hospital and meet Dr. Sundari? She's the infertility expert and we could have a chat. Then you wouldn't then have to wait ages for an appointment in England.'

I could see the sense in my sister's offer. Of course it would be quicker and easier talking informally to her colleague, but even so I didn't want to go. If there was something wrong, I preferred not to know yet. However, I couldn't think of a sensible reason to refuse. I didn't have any plans for the morning and her hospital was very close. My sister would take me on her way to work. So I gave in.

It was a ten-minute drive, and in another ten minutes, we were sitting opposite the gynaecologist.

First she asked how long we had been trying and what my cycles were like.

'It's not unusual at all,' the doctor said. 'She should give it a year. With today's stressful lifestyles and busy lives, it can take quite long.' She was addressing my sister, instead of me. I was being talked about in the third person almost as if I wasn't there.

'I travel quite a lot,' I added.

'Yes, anything like that can add to the time and if her husband travels too, it's more likely she is missing those vital days.'

I didn't tell her I had been calculating the best days for conception for the last few months, complete with an ovulation kit. I preferred to hear the theory that it was down to time and getting the date right. Of course, nothing was wrong with me. How could there be given what had I had been through already?

'We advise women to take folic acid while trying to conceive.' She spoke as if addressing an audience. There were others in the room, assistants and nurses though no one had introduced them to me.

'I did have folic acid but, you know, since I wasn't conceiving, I stopped,' I said. It was true. The folic acid tablets felt like a mockery after the first five to six months. When they had run out a month ago, I hadn't renewed supplies.

Dr. Sundari rolled her eyes in displeasure. 'This is the problem with these people. They have good habits but don't maintain them.' I assumed *these people* meant all patients. I was beginning to get annoyed with her attitude, treating the patient as ignorant and inferior to the doctor who dispensed the golden truth. I was reminded of the times I had met doctors in Calcutta with the same god-like attitude.

'Can you tell us what we need to do to find out what might be wrong? She lives in London, but since she is here, I wanted to see if you could possibly offer a diagnosis,' my sister said.

'London! Too long waiting times!' The doctor shook her head. 'I worked in London for a while you know.'

'Yes, that's why I brought her to meet you. You will understand.

Could she have some tests done today?' My sister was laying on the charm to get me a diagnosis as quickly as possible.

'What we normally do is test the man for sperm counts and other abnormalities. Then we check the woman.'

I gave my sister a triumphant smile as if to say, I told you I knew the process.

Looking away, my sister continued, 'Her husband isn't here. He's still in Odisha so is there anything you could do for her today?'

'My husband has been tested and his results are normal,' I piped up, but they ignored me. I could easily have not been in the room.

'Well, what day of her cycle is it?'

My sister looked at me.

'It's kind of in the middle.' My answer didn't please the doctor.

'If she was in the first phase or the last phase of her cycle, I could have asked for some blood tests. Let her come back on day twenty-one of her cycle. Following the blood tests, we recommend a pelvic ultrasound and then we can think about possible problems.'

'She is leaving in two days,' my sister said. I was pretty gleeful. It meant I could go home now and think about the tests later.

'Then there is no use. She has to come on the ...'

'Can't she have the scan now? The blood tests can be done later, at the appropriate time in her cycle,' my sister persisted.

The doctor considered for a moment. 'Well, I could put in a request for a scan certainly. You can take it to the scanning department.'

'Where is the scanning department?' I asked.

'Just the next floor up,' my sister said. She looked determined.

She was a sincere doctor and she made it her mission to have me tested.

Dr. Sundari wrote on a form and handed it to me. 'Show this at the reception upstairs. You may have to wait a while. But meet me with the results before you leave.'

On the way out, I said, 'Do we really want to do this? It's almost lunchtime and I wanted to go to Fab India. I just need one of those stoles you know. I can go back to England and have these tests done. The diagnostic process is the same everywhere.'

'It won't be a very long wait and considering that we are already in the hospital, we may as well. But if you really think you can have all these tests done as quickly in England.'

She seemed to be crumbling under the weight of my protests. The temptation to go home for lunch and a siesta was overwhelming. Did I really need to spend an afternoon in the hospital when nothing was wrong with me? After our experience last time, I didn't want to have anything to do with hospitals and doctors in India. I knew it was irrational, yet my heart was full of fear and it was hard for me to be there without feeling a sense of helplessness and anger. If I gave in and agreed to having tests now, that meant I'd accepted I had a problem. My irrational next thought was that I would in fact have a problem if they tested for one. SCID hung on my back like a stone and I didn't want to even think about yet more weights. I would be able to rationalise my hesitation much later. At that moment, I didn't want to know. I only wanted to enjoy the last couple of days of my holiday with my parents and sister's family. Once back in London, I would go through the recommended tests. On the other hand, I might become pregnant very soon, and none of this would matter. But the inevitable conversation with my mother when we reached home flashed through my mind. She would ask what the doctor had said and I would have to say nothing, because they needed to run more tests. She would ask when the tests were scheduled. And I would confess, I hadn't wanted to wait an hour for an ultrasound because I wanted to go shopping and come home instead. Her face would fall. I could hear her disappointed voice, 'Only an hour's wait? You could have had the scan and still gone out later. It would have put our minds to rest. Why didn't you?' She would be tense and worried and having made her point, would leave the room, only to come back and start all over again.

And at that point, I knew I too would ask myself, why didn't you? When given the chance to find out if there was a problem, within an hour, why didn't you take it?

'All right then. Let's just do it,' I told my sister.

She didn't wait to hear another word. Off she marched to the fifth floor, and I followed.

7

We were still sitting there forty-five minutes later along with many others in the waiting area. Waiting in places like this always made me feel helpless – waiting for hours with an unwell baby, a hungry baby who had missed his meal, waiting to be seen by arrogant doctors who charged the earth and didn't help. Standing in crowded rooms, again one among thousands, like we did for our baby's passport. Standing for hours and hours and being treated like anybody or nobody. The message was clear: we have too many people to think and worry about so one more makes no difference. What if a baby dies? Or a baby isn't born? It means nothing – for here in these waiting rooms you are nothing. And you are supposed to accept this quietly and passively because this is how it works. This would always be the way. How else can more than a billion people be managed?

I tried to shake myself out of this despair. I reminded myself that it wasn't the same situation as before. I didn't have an unwell baby. Nothing was wrong with me. I was leaving India in two days. Before my thoughts could get darker and more rebellious, it was my turn.

The technician handed me a robe. 'Change there.' She pointed at an area in a corner of the large room.

In the corner I could see the waiting area where the millions waited patiently – and needless to say, they could see me.

'How am I supposed to change here?' I grumbled. 'Don't they have better facilities?'

'Is there a cubicle or something?' my sister asked politely.

The nurse looked around blankly.

'Oh well, I will manage,' I scowled.

Later, on the examining table, the nurse put cool gel on my lower stomach and ran a cold metal probe over it, sometimes applying considerable pressure. It was slightly uncomfortable but not too bad. I watched my insides come alive on the screen. I was fully convinced nothing could be wrong. Concentric circles, the probe pushing, some more greyish circles. The radiologist paused for a moment and asked my sister, 'Has she ever had endometriosis?'

I had never heard this term. I searched my brain – what on earth was endometriosis? The name didn't ring any bells, not even from the far past. I knew my sister well. I knew her every expression. The familiar face I had grown up with had frozen at the question.

'No, never,' she replied.

'Well, she has endometriosis now.' The radiologist pointed at some blurry shapes on the screen.

'What is endometriosis?' I mouthed, when I finally caught my sister's eye. She had been looking at the screen or at the radiologist. Anywhere but me.

She shrugged. 'It's a cause of infertility.' Then turning to the radiologist, she asked, 'Where is it?' That seemed an odd thing to ask. Wasn't it always in the same part of the body?

'There are large chocolate cysts in both ovaries. But here, in this right ovary, it's not clear whether this is a chocolate cyst. It's massive, almost looks solid.' My sister and the radiologist exchanged worried glances. I didn't know what a chocolate cyst was but if there was a solid cyst in an ovary, even I guessed that could be a problem.

'You might need to have a blood test as well,' the technician said.

'We will meet Dr. Sundari now. We will ask her.'

I changed back into my clothes, this time without protest, and we walked back to the doctor.

'Why does this thing...endo whatever, happen?' I asked my sister.

'It's one of those diseases where the cause isn't very clear. Something to do with periods when the blood, instead of flowing out, flows inwards and leaves deposits inside the uterus. But I didn't know it could affect both the ovaries without occurring in the uterus too. How unusual.' she said, looking at the report. I didn't know if it was bad or good to have it in the ovaries instead of the uterus.

Dr. Sundari saw us again very quickly. She looked shocked. She hadn't expected I would come back with something like this.

'Big chocolate cysts in both ovaries,' she said, looking at the report, 'but in the right ovary, the cyst seems solid.'

'What are chocolate cysts?' I asked.

'Chocolate cysts are a characteristic of endometriosis. They are not solid, almost like a liquid chocolate, hence the name. We are not worried about those. But the solid looking one in the right ovary here needs to be tested. We need to rule out the possibility of it being cancerous. She needs to have a blood test for CA125. It's a marker for cancer. If it's high, then we recommend a biopsy of the cyst. Come back this afternoon because the blood test lab is closed now.'

'But what about the endometriosis? Will she need surgery?' my sister asked.

'She needs to have a laparoscopy. Since she is in a hurry to conceive the sooner the better. You could admit her tomorrow and we can do the procedure.'

'I am leaving the day after. I can't get admitted tomorrow,' I said.

Dr. Sundari shrugged. If it was this important, then surely I should have it done, her expression said.

'But surely you must have had some symptoms?' she asked, looking at me for only a moment. 'Painful periods? Painful intercourse?'

'No, never.' I said.

She didn't look convinced.

'I mean, I would know, wouldn't I?'

'It is strange that she has such severe endometriosis but no symptoms at all.' Her tone disbelieving, almost as if I was deliberately tricking everyone.

Driving back, my sister was quiet for a while, her face scrunched up with disbelief. 'Endometriosis…but how can you possibly have that? No one in our family has anything like this. It is not even that well known, you know.'

'Since when have I had it, do you think?' I asked, as if knowing the exact moment of onset would help somehow.

'It's hard to tell. But both the ovaries are affected quite badly. You need to have the surgery done soon. A laparoscopy is not a very complex operation.'

Back home, my mother was waiting anxiously. As I cried silently over my lunch, rice, dal and prawn curry made just the way I liked it, my sister told my mother about the diagnosis.

'But there is a cure, isn't it? It's so good that we know now.'

'Cure?! And now they are saying I also have cancer,' I said, as if it was their fault.

'They aren't saying that you have cancer. They just want to rule it out. Ovarian cancer can be serious. So we can go for the blood test in a couple of hours and I will get the results tomorrow.'

'There is no way I am going back for a blood test, cancer or not,' I said and stomped off to the bedroom. The computer sat in a corner. Again I searched another unfamiliar term.

Endometriosis – the cause unknown and without a cure. There are a number of theories. Working women are perhaps more prone or it could be genetic. The best way to stop the onslaught of the condition, in some Catch 22 travesty, is to get pregnant, except that endometriosis makes it hard to get pregnant.

Shopping and siesta forgotten, I read further. I enunciated the word – en-doh-mee-tri-o-sis – the way it should be pronounced. The name derives from endometrium which is the tissue that lines the womb. Every month, the uterus prepares itself to allow an embryo to implant itself and grow. If there is no fertilisation, the endometrium sheds itself in what we know as a period. Sometimes, no one seems to know why, the endometrium tissue finds its way into the fallopian tubes and grows outside the uterus. It behaves like the lining of the womb, thickening and bleeding every month, but without any exit for the blood so it creates adhesions and inflammation in the fallopian tubes, the ovaries and other areas of the pelvis.

The main symptom of endometriosis is severe pain. The main outcome is infertility. Common symptoms are pain during periods, during intercourse and in the lower back. Pain, pain, pain. The word was in every article I read. The usual method of diagnosis is a laparoscopy because there are no external manifestations. One form of the condition, ovarian endometriosis, can be diagnosed easily using ultrasound because chocolate cysts form in the ovaries, making it easy to diagnose. Only 15-20% of cases fall in this sub-category. This is what I seemed to have.

I imagined globules of congealed blood forming cysts in delicate ovaries, trapping eggs and not releasing them for conception. While I had none of the pain or back ache, I clearly wasn't the normal healthy person I thought I was. I had grade 3 endometriosis and both ovaries were filled with chocolate cysts, making them useless. The chocolate cysts were so called because of their colour, old blood accumulating month after month, a dark reddish brown. My condition was so rampant I needed surgery as soon as possible. Looking at pictures of cysts on the internet, I wondered if I would ever like chocolate again.

My husband was still in Odisha with his family. I called him. The last thing he was expecting was news of this magnitude. 'Not only that, they suspect it may even be cancer! I don't want to go for any more tests.' I told him after explaining what endometriosis was.

'Don't worry. You can get those tests done in England, if required.'

'What do you mean if required? Of course it's all required. Don't you get it?' The tears were coming so fast and I was angry. Angry at the doctors, the hospital, the heat, at myself and my awful bad luck. There was I worrying for years about invasive tests to check for SCID when I couldn't even conceive. I never imagined I'd have to face yet another frightening medical condition. No-one in my family had experienced problems conceiving. I came from an overpopulated country. Fertility was the problem, not infertility. Life certainly knew how to laugh at me.

I had only occasionally heard stories of infertility. A friend and her husband had been diagnosed with unexplained infertility – a condition when neither partner has a medical issue that prevents conception, yet they can't conceive. We had developed a bond, sharing our stories of loss and yearning. I used to empathise with her and feel that I was lucky because I'd conceived easily and had experienced motherhood, however briefly.

Eventually I stopped reading articles about endometriosis and went up to the terrace. The evening air was pleasantly cool. In the darkness, I sat alone and wept. *Why me? Why is this happening to me?* On his return from work, my brother-in-law came upstairs to find me. My mother followed. They tried to console me, saying everything would be all right. There was a diagnosis so there would be a solution. 'You will be fine. We are with you,' they said.

They – my parents, brother-in-law, sister, everyone – wanted me to have the blood test for cancer markers done immediately but I was adamant. I refused. They suggested I stay on. They offered support so I could have the laparoscopy in Chennai.

'You will have to wait for a long time for an appointment in the UK, whereas here you can be admitted tomorrow and have your operation the day after. The quicker they rule out cancer, the better. You can postpone your return and leave after two weeks when you are fully rested,' my sister said, persuasively.

'If it's cancer, the NHS will push me through the medical system and I will get immediate treatment. If it's not cancer, I can have the operation done privately. After all, I would pay here so I might as well pay there to have it done.' Unfortunately, I didn't have private medical insurance from the current company.

'We would be able to look after you after your surgery. How will you manage over there all on your own?'

There was some truth in that. There was no one waiting for me in London. My family's love and care was here. Yet I wanted to get back. My silent house. My work. My true self – all there. The thought of having an operation in two days in Chennai terrified me.

I sat in the guest bedroom of my sister's flat and dialled the surgery in London. I fixed an appointment with Dr. Patel for the day after we arrived in London. I hoped that Dr. Sundari and her team had made some massive mistake and the diagnosis would be different. I hoped that Dr. Patel could make everything better for me.

8

I was back in the surgery, my scans and report from India fanned out on the table. As always, Dr. Patel started by telling me a little about the condition, how it affects the body, and what treatment is available. She confirmed most of what the doctor in India had told me.

'But how does endometriosis cause infertility?' While I had read the how and what, I wasn't clear about the why.

'Neither the cause nor the effect are very clear. We believe that the cysts, these chocolate cysts which form in the uterus, create a very inhospitable environment for the eggs to live in. They don't survive long, and even if they do, they aren't released in the way they need to be to meet the sperm. Then there are a lot of adhesions and scar tissue which create further complications.'

I would need a surgical procedure to remove and clear all the adhesions and cysts in my ovaries.

'And how long will I need to wait for this?'

'The current waiting list to see a gynaecologist is a couple of months.'

In India I could have had surgery the following day. Maybe I had been wrong to come back, like everyone had said. I tried another tack.

'Don't I need an urgent appointment and a blood test to check for ovarian cancer?'

'Oh, you don't have ovarian cancer, don't worry. Chocolate cysts often have a solid appearance when they are big. You are at very low risk of ovarian cancer.'

While that made me feel better, I still wanted an appointment with the gynaecologist soon. Waiting months was not an option.

'I'll go privately.' Rather the expense than further delays.

'In that case, I will recommend you see Mr. Smith,' she said, writing in her report.

Two days later, I was given an appointment by Mr. Smith's secretary. He would see me in one of the private hospitals about ten minutes from our home.

Chelsfield hospital was at the end of a small winding country road, tucked away behind mature trees, like a Bed and Breakfast. No skyscraper, no vast, sprawling building, but a country cottage. The interior was similarly unlike a hospital. No disinfectant smells, no long, dark corridors.

'Do take a seat. Mr. Smith is running very late,' the receptionist said. Their smiles and shrugs told me that it was not unusual for Mr. Smith to be late. We had imagined we would be in and out within half an hour – after all, this was a private appointment, but this was not to be. An hour later Mr. Smith welcomed us and apologised for the delay. He was a slight, well-dressed man in a smart, dark suit and red tie, like someone I would meet at work. I remembered my confusion when the receptionist had phoned.

'I thought I had an appointment with a doctor? Why am I meeting a Mr. Smith?' I had asked.

'Mr. Smith is a surgeon,' the receptionist had explained.

'Why isn't he called Dr. Smith?'

'Because he is a surgeon,' she answered patiently.

After doing some research I understood that in England a surgeon is called Mister instead of Doctor. The first surgeons in the country were butchers with no medical qualifications. Surgery was then considered an inferior skill within medical practice.

It was hard to imagine the slightest likeness to a butcher in this gentle man who stood in front of us.

'So I was on holiday in India, and had this scan, my sister took me, she is a doctor, and they said I had endometriosis. They also said I may have cancer and they wanted me to get a blood test to check for cancer markers.' I was nervously blabbering.

'That's not a nice thing to tell you when you are on holiday, is it?' he said, very calmly. He had a curious lilting tone. His words dipped suddenly or raised in an intonation when you least expected it.

'How young are you?' he asked, making me smile. 'OK, let's get the scan done.'

A gynaecologist who did his own scans was a first for me. He drew the curtain around the table and gave me a few minutes to undress. Mr. Smith pushed a cold probe inside me, and then, shapes appeared on the screen.

'Look! These are the ovaries,' he said, as if he was seeing some wondrous thing for the first time in his life. 'You can see the follicles here.' He pointed at some large dark spaces and kept clicking, presumably to take pictures.

I was hoping his diagnosis would be different but his words were the same. 'It's quite bad endometriosis, grade 3. Cysts in both the ovaries. A clear uterus. But you are really lucky, aren't you?'

As I wondered how on earth I could be considered lucky, he

continued, 'You don't have any pain. Normally, this is a very painful condition.'

He went on to explain that I would need to have a laparoscopy. I would be given a general anesthetic and he would 'repair' the ovaries by removing the cysts. I would be able to conceive easily after that. Almost 80% of women conceived within three months of the procedure. It all sounded simple.

'And don't I need a blood test to check for cancer?'

'The CA125, an indicator for cancer, is also high with endometriosis so there's no need for a blood test. We will know if you are at risk after the operation. It's highly doubtful. I am sure the cysts are chocolate cysts. One does look a bit solid but that's due to the size.'

'So this marker would have shown up high anyway? I am so glad I didn't have the test! I would have thought I had cancer!' I said.

'That wouldn't have been very nice while on holiday, would it?' he smiled as he led us out.

We were to discuss everything and get back to him to book a date for the surgery.

I went home and read that a laparoscopy, though not as invasive as traditional surgery, was still quite complicated. They filled the stomach with carbon dioxide to blow it up. Then they made two small incisions on each side and introduced cameras. Due to the gas pumped in, there was good visibility in the whole abdominal cavity, allowing the surgeon to remove cysts or whatever else they needed to do. It took days for the stomach to return to its previous size.

At work, I explained to my manager that I needed an operation. His face took on a triumphant smile. 'I knew it! I knew something was wrong, in fact all of us did. You haven't been your usual energetic self since you have been back from India! Now we know!'

'I didn't tell them the whole truth however – a sales person wanting to get pregnant is never good news for any company. My story was that I had gone for a routine check-up that my sister had facilitated, and during an ultrasound they found I had endometriosis. They found that plausible. After all, the NHS was renowned for being slow and India was a centre for medical tourism. There was affordable, fast, quality healthcare.

Except that some conditions, like SCID, still remained largely untreatable.

9

Two weeks later, I was in the pre-surgery room, listening to the nurses asking if Mr. Smith had arrived. I had hoped to see him before the operation to feel reassured but they gave me an injection and I must have drifted off before he came in, late as always. I woke in a quiet room, light blue walls. It felt tranquil. A large window overlooked the gardens of mature trees and lush grass. I could have been on holiday. In a NHS hospital, the surgery is carried out as an outpatient procedure, but here I could stay for the night. I was in no hurry to leave. It was so restful.

'When you want to get out of bed, you must call for us.' The nurse had cautioned me not to try and walk on my own. I felt perfectly fine, however, and tried to get up to go to the bathroom in the evening. My legs were wobbly and I collapsed. I hadn't expected to feel so light headed. I pressed the bell and the nurse arrived, quietly admonishing me. She helped me to the bathroom.

'It's only the first few steps. Soon you will be fine.'

They brought dinner to the room and the next morning, a delicious breakfast in bed. It had snowed the night before and a sheet of white cloaked the trees and grass. It felt like a new beginning, a beautiful beginning. Nothing could go wrong in this idyllic world. I read my book and felt my eyes close. I was feeling so relaxed.

Mr. Smith came to see me. 'You are fine now. I have repaired you.' he said cheerfully. 'You can put in your order for a boy or girl, or twins!'

When my husband came to take me home, I said I was in no hurry. Perhaps seeing how relaxed and settled I was, they served me my lunch, telling me I could leave when I wanted to.

'We must leave now,' my husband said, when I'd finished eating. 'We really must. You can't stay any longer!'

I reluctantly said goodbye to the quiet un-hospital-like retreat.

At home, I had to spend most of the day on the red sofa in the living room. Brisk walking was not recommended for several days and I could feel the discomfort of a significantly bloated stomach when I did try to walk. Since they classified laparoscopy as minor surgery I wondered if the doctors had ever had a similar procedure. The blown up stomach took two or three weeks to settle down. The keyhole incisions meant you needed to walk slowly and rest as much as you could. Recovery wasn't in a day as I had imagined.

A huge vase of flowers arrived from the office. Lavish lilies, gladioli, roses, and a card with wishes. I spent my days reading and watching television. My husband was out at work so I could enjoy quiet days. I went back to work after a few days and saw the concern in my colleagues' eyes. I imagined the questions they wanted to ask, but didn't. Was I all right? Had I recovered? Was I pregnant? Would I continue wearing such baggy clothes? Would my walking improve?

When I went to Mr. Smith for my follow up appointment, he said again, 'You can put in your order for twins if you want to. I have repaired the ovaries. It's all clear now.'

'And any more worries about cancer?' I asked, still concerned.

'No, they were all chocolate cysts as we had expected. Some

were very dense which is why they appeared solid on the scan. See you in the maternity clinic!' he said cheerfully as he waved us goodbye.

Finally, I was whole. It would happen soon. I could feel it.

10

Months passed. Nothing. More visits. More scans.

'But the follicles are here, ready to be released' or 'It's all clear' or 'But I repaired you', Mr. Smith would say in utter disbelief.

He started me on Clomid cycles, little pills to be taken for a certain number of days at certain times of the month. Little pills, packing promises and hope.

I had to travel to Brussels for a conference during my three fertile days of the month. My husband came over for one night so we could maximise our chances on Clomid, instead of waiting for yet another month. Over dinner in the restaurant in Central Square, we dreamed that in a year's time we would visit Brussels with our baby, definitely a girl this time. We would come back to this very restaurant, stay overnight and walk through the lazy squares, little fingers entwined in ours. Our baby girl – I was so sure, with my prayers, I would have a girl – would be ours very soon.

A couple of weeks later, there was the trickle of blood in the office bathroom. When I went back to my desk, eyes patted and dried, one of my colleagues looked up. Whether she knew anything was amiss, I had no idea.

I was getting desperate. Was it ever going to happen?

Around me, the entire world was producing babies. Everyone, anyone. The blush, the refusal of the proffered glass of wine. It was becoming so commonplace that I was on edge whenever we met couples. My tears rose angry, my tears rose sad. When yet another friend invited us for a child's first birthday, I muttered, 'These people, unimpressive, ordinary, why are they all reproducing and bringing children like themselves into the world? Boring, mundane people.'

I liked my friends, I liked their children, but I didn't like the person I was becoming. *What a failure you are! A dead child. An unconceived child.* What could be wrong with me? After what I had gone through, surely I deserved things to go smoothly this time round. *Pray harder. There are enough Gods to choose from so take your pick.*

To make matters worse, I wasn't happy with my job. Though I was successful and met my sales target, the company didn't seem a good long-term option. There was no salary increase, or promotions, or a career path, however well one did. Most of my colleagues were looking for a change. Since my career decisions were tied to my personal goal of having a baby, I was weighing up time to establish myself before becoming pregnant with staying where I was, without career prospects, and trying for a baby now. But I wasn't getting pregnant so I might as well get something more out of my work. A new job seemed the answer to my problems.

It was around this time, when I was dithering, that I met one of my ex-colleagues and he told me that his company was looking for hard-working, successful people like me.

Very soon, I had a meeting with the sales head.

There were several things that tempted me to accept the subsequent offer, including a higher salary and travelling only within England. I could work from home and commute to the office once every week or two. I would manage one large account, rather than having to forage for new business all over Europe and Africa. Sales was not an easy job but I was determined to prove myself an excellent sales person. Women were rare in technology sales and Indian women even rarer. I was determined to stay the course and balance my career with a family. This new company, which was a large Indian organisation, was an ideal place to be if I was thinking about a baby. It was much larger than my previous company so I would feel less guilty about taking maternity leave.

Even though I had just joined a new company, I had no intention of stopping trying for a child. If I became pregnant soon, I would be able to manage a pregnancy and the demands of the job. My days were much less stressful. No running up the hill to catch the overground train to London Bridge, no squeezing into the crowded Jubilee line, no grabbing a sandwich lunch. With this new, less punishing schedule, it would now only be a matter of weeks.

I was completely wrong on both counts. I couldn't have chosen a worse company or a worse time to join. There had been a change of management and they had a new head of Europe, the boss of the person who recruited me. Combining an old school whip-the-sales-person approach with a new world aggression, he found in me his perfect target. The only woman in a team of older men, the only person from a background of international companies, the only one who did not worship the ground he trod on, I was on the receiving end of his abusive threats. As Clomid cycles came and went, and every month resulted in failure, I attended sales meetings where my weak pipeline or my presentations were mocked. I had been the most successful revenue earner in my previous organisation. Now I was the one who could do nothing right. My previous offices were based in London so there was no reason to drive to work. Now we lived in the suburbs but my office and my customers were in distant towns so I was being urged to get behind the wheel and taunted for not being able to do so. I had been trying to pass my driving test for a while but even after countless lessons, I failed my test every time. The instructor's frustration and anger at my inability to master manoeuvres collided with the mockery within the workplace and the utter desolation of the monthly cycle.

Every month we were back with Mr. Smith. Three cycles had gone by.

'I don't understand why it's not happening,' he would say. 'Look, you can see the follicles, waiting to be released.' He would pause with the ultrasound probe to show me healthy follicles and eggs. Lying on the now familiar scan table, I would look at the picture of my ovaries and wonder. When?

Scan over, I would get up and ask yet again, 'Is everything normal?'

'Yes, it all looks perfectly normal. It should happen soon. I will see you in the hospital.' His goodbyes still spoke of hope.

Since he practised both in the NHS and privately, the plan was that when I eventually became pregnant I would transfer to the gynaecology ward but still under his care.

My friend from Netmums sent me two healing stones, a pink one for fertility, a green for health. The energy from the stones will help you, she said. While she conceived easily, she also miscarried easily, within days sometimes. We wrote to each other, sharing the pain of what wasn't happening, and what happened but didn't stay.

Most women conceive within three to six months after having a laparoscopic procedure. The chances start to fall after that and, depending on the severity of the endometriosis, they can fall still further.

With each passing month, my chance of conceiving dropped. I carried on reading and doing my research. One article had depressing statistics that stayed in my head. The chance of pregnancy with grade 3 endometriosis was less than 1% without treatment and 1-2% after treatment. With fertility drugs and IVF it rose to only 35%.

The numbers were ruling out the possibility of a natural conception.

11

During this period, I found it painful to hear from friends and family that they had terminated their pregnancies. They gave such trivial reasons for doing so.

One couple told me that it wasn't the right time because they planned a gap of two years between their children. Another woman with teenage daughters was ashamed to admit that the pregnancy was a mistake, and decided to terminate. A third friend had planned to have no more than two children and aborted their 'third mistake'.

I live in an extremely fertile world of fornicating rabbits, I thought, in increasingly frequent, bitter moments. *I live in a world where gifts are given to people who are happy to let them go,* I thought, in more charitable moods. It was harder and harder to carry on in this normal world of working couples whose lives revolved around planning for babies, having babies, celebrating birthdays and thinking about children's futures. Without a child in the house, I wondered what the point of a home was. I thought of doing more with my life. Trekking in Machu Picchu perhaps? What could I do which would be impossible if I was pregnant?

We thought of adoption but found out that the process was long and complex. We could adopt in England or abroad. In England, after the necessary home checks, we would be placed on a waiting list. Our local borough warned us that our chances of finding a suitable child was very low as we lived in a primarily Caucasian area. Any children of Asian descent – and matching parents to children according to ethnicity was mandatory – would be Muslims and we would need to raise the child in the Islamic faith. Any children available for adoption would be older, at least three or four years old. In India babies are abandoned on the roads, often the children of single mothers, often girls. There are enough babies to go round, people assured me. But international adoption was an expensive and long process. A home study to get approved as prospective adopters could cost up to ten thousand pounds. Once we were approved, we would be registered in the country where we would adopt, in our case India, and placed on a waiting list. It was a government rule that only after a child had been turned down by three Indian couples could he or she be offered to adopters from outside India.

One morning, in a fit of desperation, I called an Indian orphanage. They reaffirmed what I had read. Families could visit orphanages and 'choose a child,' and could reject on grounds as superficial as skin colour. Darker children were less sought after, as were disabled or mentally challenged children. The children who were placed abroad mostly had illnesses that could be treated in another country. The adoption process would take at least two years and there was no guarantee of success. The road ahead seemed rocky to say the least and I was reluctant to start on a process that could end in disappointment after all I had been through. Adoption seemed an even tougher process with all the complex legal regulations. We abandoned that idea for the moment.

We went to India a year later to see our families. My parents had moved to Pondicherry. Just as the British had left their mark across Indian cities with the architecture and names of roads, Pondicherry was marked by Frenchness, from the roads named after French lords to the French eateries in the small town. There was a distinct, cosmopolitan air. It was my favourite place in India, even though the last time I had been here was when I was trying to get over the death of my baby. I wasn't born there, never lived there, yet it felt like home. There was something very spiritual about the place, with people coming to live around the ashram of The Mother and Sri Aurobindo. They were like-minded people who believed in alternative therapies, in natural healing, in art, in the unconventional.

My mother hesitantly asked if I would be willing to meet some of the alternative healers. I agreed; I was prepared to try, to ask, to seek. If nothing else, it might quieten the devastating restlessness in me.

I visited a Reiki healer, Sushmita. She listened patiently to my story, of the genes passed on without my knowledge, of my body's refusal to conceive. She asked me to pray, not to The Mother, but to Sri Aurobindo.

'But why is that? I don't want a boy.' It was more usual for Indian women to want a boy – a blessing in ancient times was, *Putravati Bhava, may you bear sons.*

'It is not that. It is because I feel you need to pray to a strong, masculine force.'

She suggested two Reiki sessions a day because she said she felt several blockages in my system. Her palms were warm as she pressed them over my body, praying all the while. I went every morning and evening for the rest of the week I was in Pondicherry. She lit a candle and I lay on the small bed, trying to immerse myself in positive energy and thought.

'It will take time, but it will happen,' she concluded. 'I think you will have a boy.'

'But that brings the possibility of SCID.'

'It will be OK.'

Next was a friendly neighbor, Saira, who practised palmistry. She held both my hands, traced the lines and said, 'You will have children for sure. It will take time though.'

It's taking a hell of a lot of time, I thought. My friends are celebrating the birthdays of their first children and some have moved on to the second.

'How much longer?!'

'It will take time, but it will happen,' she said.

I met Saidev, a guru who practised Tantra. He had an ashram where people from all over the world visited. He told me, 'The baby who went away is creating a blockage. He really loved his parents...and his soul is there, wanting to come back. It will happen.' I imagined souls hanging like crystal baubles somewhere in an astral place until they could come back to the earth. 'Pray. Have faith,' he said.

I wondered if there could be any truth in such a theory. Could my baby have loved me so much that his soul wanted to come back to me? Could his soul be waiting to return to the world and preventing another from coming to me?

I preferred to believe that the little baby who had come and gone had wanted to go. After reading so many different theories, I believed strongly that the soul chooses its path. Hindu philosophy believes in the cycle of rebirth with more than one life for a soul. It was born over and over, living many lives, dying many deaths, until fulfilled Nirvana[10] was achieved. Would any

---

10 Nirvana: salvation, freedom from the cycle of birth and death

baby choose to die? Would a soul want to complete a long life in a short time, living the equivalent of several lives in one? This theory helped me believe that my soul had asked for the challenges, making it stronger and more patient. It helped me believe that God or a Divine Grace worked with our souls to help remove the knots in our destinies. I was learning all this to bring me closer to my own path of self-realisation

I met Anurakta, an Englishman who had been living in India for forty-five years. He was known for predicting the future using a pendulum. He lived alone in a large house, in a leafy part of town. An entire room in his house was filled with Hindu idols. He looked after the deities; Krishna, Hanuman, Ganesh and others, clothing them, making garlands of marigolds and jasmines. It reminded me of the dolls I looked after when I was a child. He met us in his front room and we sat cross-legged on a mat in front of him. A delicate mini-pendulum hung between his hands. I was to ask him three questions and he would meditate, the pendulum swinging on its trajectory. Then he would write answers on a piece of paper. I only had one question and I would have preferred to ask it three times, but he insisted on three. My first question was about my job and if I had chosen the right career. My second question was whether I would ever have a child. My third whether it would be a boy or girl. He sat still with his eyes closed, the pendulum moving gently from side to side. Then he wrote the answers on a sheet of paper and handed it to me – brief answers in sprawling writing. I was in the right job. I would have a child. It would be a boy.

'When? When will it happen?'

'It will take time,' he said, parroting the answers of all the others, 'but it will happen. A boy.'

A boy? Aren't any of you listening?

'She doesn't want a boy. You know there are problems,' my mother said as if she read my mind.

'Don't worry, it will all be well,' he said. He was quiet after that, moving back into his meditation, a gesture that we could go.

As we walked out, I looked back at him. A round face, a serious man in a vest and a blue dhoti. He didn't look at all English. Years of living in India had made his soul Indian and now it was mirrored in his face.

I met Dr. Rai who practised the occult. People said he could predict the future and even make things come true. All the conditions I carried like baggage – SCID, endometriosis – made more sense to him because of his medical background. He observed me for a while to study my chakras so he could detect any imbalances or blockages. Then he sat silently for a while. He too said it would surely happen one day but that it would be a girl. He advised me to manage my diet and to stop eating wheat to control the endometriosis.

'But I can't,' I later complained at home. 'A sandwich is the best I can do for lunch. Most of the cereals I eat are wheat based.'

'You don't have to do everything they say,' my parents consoled.

By now my sister had a baby girl, a few months old. I went to Bangalore to visit them. It wasn't lost on me that I had started planning and trying long before she did, and here I was with nothing. She told me about a temple where couples faced with infertility went to beseech the Gods and were always rewarded. She knew I didn't believe in rituals so it was with hesitation that she asked me to go. It couldn't hurt, I thought. There was almost nothing I wouldn't do to give myself a chance. So a trip was arranged to the temple of the *Navaneeta Krishna*, the baby Krishna, on the outskirts of Bangalore.

We drove along quiet roads. My brother-in-law, sister and their baby girl were with me. The temple was busy, so many parents here to pray, so many parents in similar situations. Many were buying little statues of the crawling Krishna from the small stalls outside the temples.

'See, they're offering these as benediction for wishes to come true,' my sister said. 'This temple is revered.'

I noticed many of the families had little girls with them.

'Are you sure they aren't all praying for a son?' I asked 'They seem to have daughters already so why are they all praying to Krishna?'

'No, I've been told it's for any child,' my sister replied, but she looked worried.

We went inside and as I bowed to the shrine, I asked yet again, and again, please let me have a healthy child soon. please God of many names, whether The Mother or Sri Aurobindo or Krishna or Shiva or Durga.

Outside the temple, I stopped for a minute at one of the stalls and the seller held out idols on his hand.

'Rs.150 only,' he said. A black statue of Krishna crawling with a little pot of butter in one hand.

I bought it. 'Krishna is such a cute God! But if I place this idol with my other gods at home, it doesn't mean I am asking for a boy, right?'

'Not at all,' my sister assured me.

'You can always ask Krishna to send his friend Radha instead,' my mother explained when I asked her on the phone.

We came back to London, God in the suitcase, my body calmer, my mind at rest.

Some days later, I went with my husband to a conference in Paris. During the day, left to myself to explore this city I loved, I visited the museums and strolled through the parks. I found Rodin's Thinker in the museum and wondered if his thoughts were as much of a quagmire as mine were. In Notre Dame, I lit a candle and prayed to the Mother Mary and Jesus.

'You know how I feel, you as a mother, give me your blessings,' I prayed.

12

Months passed. Nothing happened. Another acronym started flashing across my mind. Was it time to think of IVF[11]?

We booked an appointment with the fertility expert we saw before, Mr. Smith, and arrived with a list of questions. Should we carry on with Clomid? What about other treatments? Should we have IVF? Most fertility doctors carried out a few cycles of IUI (Intra-Uterine Insemination) but Mr. Smith saw no need. He thought the possibility of success was low so it would be a waste of time and effort. His suggestion was to go ahead with IVF.

IVF was a possible solution to the problem of conception but what about SCID? At Guy's we had been told there were three options: Pre-implantation genetic testing (PGD) when a girl embryo would be placed in the uterus, PGD which included IVF since fertilisation took place outside the body, and then embryo selection. Now that we were thinking of IVF, should we also be considering embryo selection? Should we have a PGD instead?

There were two reasons we were not enthusiastic. First, PGD had an even lower success rate than IVF. It would also be very expensive, done privately, with no guaranteed outcome. Secondly, while specialist centres like Guy's in London had a licence to do

11 IVF: In-vitro fertilsation, or colloquially known as test-tube baby

embryo selection for medical reasons like SCID, Mr. Smith didn't. Should we go to Guy's? Or stay with Mr. Smith? He would start me on an IVF cycle the next month. If successful and I conceived, we would have an early gender scan and, depending on the result, we could opt for a test to check for SCID. Back and forth we went, trying to decide on the best plan. Finally we decided on an IVF cycle with Mr. Smith to tackle the problem of conception. Boy, girl or SCID would be the next problem to worry about but until I conceived, none of that applied. Mr. Smith had a high success rate with IVF so we were maximising our chances.

A part of me didn't believe in pumping drugs into the body or forcing conception but I told myself, just the once, just one try, and if that didn't work, then we would embark on the adoption process.

It was summer 2006 and my parents were visiting us for the first time. We planned to take them to Paris and to the Lake District. While we could have started the first cycle, I felt it wouldn't be fair to them to embark on IVF with me possibly unwell and full of drugs. So we decided to begin once they left.

Meanwhile, Mr. Smith prescribed two blood tests to check the possible success rate of the procedure. One came back normal and the other said I had a high factor of Protein C. We had no idea what that meant but knew that Mr. Smith would explain in due course. Dr. Patel gave me a prescription for the fertility drugs. I went to Boots on the high street. The woman behind the counter took a while to collect the various items from drawers and cupboards. The pile grew.

'IVF stuff. I am having one next month,' I smiled at her.

'Good luck! It will be so worth it.'

'You think so? I mean…does it work really?'

'Of course! And you will be so happy you did it.'

I needed reassurance from everyone. I would probably have asked a duck if one had swum past just then.

The drugs now sat in my fridge. A whole set of bottles on the lower shelf. A set of syringes for the drugs. I would breathe some fertility into myself with the help of the nasal sprays.

Two days before we were to leave for the Lake District with my parents, I noticed a spot on my collarbone. It looked like a small boil. I didn't think much of it until the next morning when there was another on my face.

'Looks odd, doesn't it? Is this chicken pox?' I asked my mother.

It seemed innocuous enough. I had to go to a meeting at work but whilst there, I could feel more spots erupting on my face.

'Do you think I have chicken pox?' I asked my colleague.

While he, concerned, asked how I felt and whether I had a fever, the bully boss heard me and was annoyed. Later, he would use it against me, 'She came to a meeting with chicken pox. She actually asked us if she had chicken pox!'

By the evening, the spots had spread all over my face, neck and shoulders.

When I was eleven, my sister (then fourteen) caught chicken pox. She had a bad strain and suffered for a couple of weeks. The spots left scars and for months my mother was concocting pastes and lotions. Someone suggested that I bathe in a mixture of *juwani*[12] and *torani*[13] An old wives tale said that if you bathed in this mixture, the goddess of chickenpox wouldn't enter it because your body wasn't clean. The five other children, our

12 Juwani: Ajwain seeds
13 Torani: water in which rice has been cooked, left to ferment

immediate neighbours with whom we played with every day, also got it, one after the other. Miraculously, I was the only one who didn't, even though my sister and I shared a room. So for years after, whenever there was chicken pox going round, my mother reminded me of my preventative bath. I had my own protection against the disease. Unlike in England where people tried to get chicken pox as a child, in India it was best avoided.

Now as an adult, there had been no warning or news of anyone contracting chickenpox and I hadn't done my superstitious treatment for whatever it was worth.

When I called the hospital to discuss the blood test result and mentioned my chicken pox, there was immediate concern. This was one of the deadliest diseases for a pregnant woman. They would need me to get completely well before they could carry out the IVF procedure.

Much to my chagrin, the cycle had to be delayed for two months, another disappointment when I was in a hurry to start this journey.

Chicken pox took its toll. Even so, and with spots all over my face, we went to the Lake District, always so tranquil and beautiful. We went to Paris, visited the museums, and also took my parents on a walking tour of the houses The Mother had lived in, before she had come to Pondicherry. My pictures from those days show me in a cap and long scarves and sunglasses.

It was 2006. We had been living in the UK for five years and having passed our naturalisation test, were ready to be sworn in as British citizens. My parents attended the ceremony. During all my years in India, I had never dreamed of, or even wanted, such a day. Then I was a proud national with no wish to leave my country of birth, my motherland. Yet here I stood, fumbling

161

a little with nerves while saying the oath, spots all over my face but no confusion in my heart. I had worked hard for this moment. It had seemed like an impossible dream, yet this day had arrived. I had earned the right to stay forever in the country where I would bring up my child. For me, this day was momentous, a culmination of my hopes, despair and dreams. The oath taker guessed nothing and saw nothing that was beyond the ordinary.

13

In August, a few days after my parents left, I realised my period was late. I was never late. If anything, my monthly cycles were arriving earlier and earlier, bringing increased frustration with them and preventing me from dreaming that this could be the month. I let two more days pass. Still no sign of the familiar blood. I didn't dare hope. At the weekend, though, on impulse, I decided to get out the pregnancy test which I still had from the days of buying ovulation kits. I told myself the chances of a positive result were miniscule but a drowning person will clutch at a straw, as they say. I rummaged for the test in the drawer, read the instructions and carefully followed them. For a moment, I didn't dare look. Then I summoned the courage to open my eyes and there it was. Two dark pink lines. I re-read the instructions. Two dark pink lines indicate a pregnancy. There was no mistake. I went downstairs to my husband who was watching television. I showed him the stick with its lines. I couldn't say anything. Of course he didn't understand – until he looked at my face.

This was a surprise. More than that, a miracle. We were utterly astounded and amazed.

I looked at the drugs sitting next to the orange juice in the fridge. Would I not need these now? I kept looking at the stick in case I had imagined those lines. It remained resolutely dark pink.

On Monday, I went to Dr. Patel for confirmation. She did a quick test and looked jubilant. If a doctor could have hugged her patient, she would have.

'This is a miracle baby!' she said.

'Are you sure? Is the test 100% accurate?'

'A positive can sometimes show as a negative, but when it's a positive, that is it!'

She was smiling so hard; I could have been her sister.

'What shall I do with the IVF drugs?' I asked.

'Keep them for now, just in case. But forget about them. Relax and enjoy your pregnancy,' she said.

We knew that we would only be able to relax once we knew the chances of SCID reoccurring but we had a few weeks still before the test that would check the foetus.

Later, we met Mr. Smith.

'I knew it! I told you I had repaired it perfectly. I will now see you in the maternity ward.' He seemed hugely relieved, even though it meant he had lost an IVF patient and the associated fee.

Finally, I was pregnant. Now for the real journey, and the real struggle. It was time to worry about prenatal diagnostic tests, the baby's gender, and to wonder which way the dice had rolled this time. I felt positive. It was a girl, surely.

Mr. Smith told us that we could have a scan to check the gender at fourteen weeks. If it was a girl, we needn't worry. If it was a boy, we could still think of having amniocentesis around sixteen weeks. CVS was ruled out because the test was invasive and carried a high risk of miscarriage which we all rejected for this precious miracle baby. Everything possible would be done. The message from both my doctors was clear. I was in safe hands.

It was around this time that I had a driving test. Over a year I'd tried several times and still hadn't passed. One of the manoeuvres was the emergency stop, which meant you had to brake suddenly, and potentially it could be a risk if you were pregnant. I had read that somewhere. So I told the examiner rather proudly before we started, 'I need to let you know that I am about ten weeks pregnant so I will not be able to carry out the emergency stop procedure even if you ask me to.'

'OK, I will keep that in mind, though we cannot guarantee what manoeuvres we can and can't ask you to undertake in the test today,' he replied, politically correct.

He didn't ask me to do it. I passed the test. My baby was already lucky for me, I thought, delighted.

Never did I expect the next four weeks to be so eventful: repeated episodes of spotting, scans to check my baby's heart was still beating, time off work. And I certainly never imagined that at fourteen weeks and five days, on a Thursday evening after dinner when I took my plate to the kitchen sink, there would be a sudden whoosh and a pool of sticky gel would spill over the kitchen floor. I never imagined googling a frightening condition called PPROM – premature rupture of membranes.

Which is why, I reasoned, as I lay in bed that fateful evening, that this ruptured membrane stuff couldn't be happening to me. This time around, everything was supposed to be perfect. Why? Surely I deserved it! After everything I had been through.

SECTION 4 – WATER – PATIENCE

1

As I lay burning with fever that Thursday night in October 2006, in my home in London, I prayed my miracle baby would be fine. Four long years and this was my 'long awaited, much prayed for, nothing can possibly go wrong baby.' With the Clexane injections and progesterone pessaries prescribed by Mr. Smith, I had expected to have a worry-free second trimester. My nuchal scan at twelve weeks had been perfect. My baby had shown a normal weight. During the scan, the doctor had said that the baby looked happy.

The minute the hands of the clock moved to 8 a.m. I called Claire, the midwife. She said I needed to see Dr. Patel and then Mr. Smith. If it was an amniotic fluid rupture, which she hoped it wasn't, there was little she could do.

I asked for an emergency appointment with Dr. Patel and she saw me within the hour. As I described what had happened, her face lost colour.

'It's got to be a urinary tract infection. Think back. Are you sure it was fluid? Since you have a temperature as well, there's a strong chance you have a water infection.'

I wanted to believe her. I wanted to forget that the previous evening had ever happened. I wanted to have a water infection but I could still remember the gel-like liquid. And I would have known if I had lost control of my bladder. I didn't disagree with her. I hoped that Dr. Patel knew my body better than I did. She took a urine sample. Frowning, she drew pictures of the womb and explained the functions of amniotic fluid.

'If the sac has ruptured...well...that's the worst possible outcome. But how can that be? This is a miracle baby! Let's wait for the test results and see what Mr. Smith says. I will contact him now and get you an appointment today.' His clinic was in one of the other private hospitals that day.

I went home. There was no further leakage and I began to think that maybe the nightmare was over. In the afternoon, Dr. Patel called to say I had an appointment in the evening. My husband came back from work and we went together. It was the first time Mr. Smith didn't smile when he greeted us.

When I lay down on the examining table, the scan showed a fuzzy picture. Without the nourishing fluid around it, my baby couldn't even be seen.

'This is not a nice thing to happen, is it?' Mr. Smith said, face pale.

'But why did it happen?' I asked.

'No one knows for sure why an amniotic sac ruptures. I suspect you have contracted an infection. I will need to take a swab but I will start you on some strong antibiotics anyway while we wait for the results.'

'Is this...is it PPROM?' my husband asked. I knew he was hoping that the internet research he was always dead against was wrong.

'Yes, Preterm Premature Rupture of Membranes. PPROM. The amniotic sac bursts and the fluid leaks out long before viability.' He told us what I had already heard before from Dr. Patel.

Mr. Smith suggested that I call King's or ask Dr. Patel to ask for an immediate scan. I already had an appointment for the following week for the gender determination scan but with this new development, Mr. Smith was sure they would see me immediately. He asked me to come back after the scan.

When I called King's and told them the problem, sure enough, they gave me an appointment for the next day.

2

At King's College, my husband and I waited in trepidation for my turn. It was five days since the leakage and there'd been hardly anything more. I hoped the scan would be encouraging. I sat there willing it to be positive. The waiting area was full and it was almost two hours before I was called.

We went into a large room with the ultrasound scanner on one side. I described the incident yet again to the small team. The doctors looked worried.

'But since then, there has been no more leaking,' I said, with eager hope. Maybe they would say that it wasn't so bad. All would be well.

'The reason there is no more leaking is that there is nothing left to leak,' the doctor told me grimly. 'Look at that,' she continued, moving the probe on my stomach. I couldn't see anything, none of the little whorls of previous scans, no familiar shape we knew was the head, no typical foetus outline like you see in movies. It was fuzzy. It was dark. 'Since there is hardly any fluid left, we can't see the baby clearly. Although the lack of fluid and the early stage of the pregnancy makes it hard to confirm, I think it looks like it's a boy.'

I looked at my husband. This couldn't be! It couldn't be another boy. I was meant to have a girl this time!

'Are you sure it's a boy?' I asked, suddenly angry with this doctor, as if it was her fault.

'We can't be a hundred percent certain under the circumstances but from what we see now, yes, it's a boy.'

Once again, we were told about the very high risks of my situation. There was no treatment for prematurely ruptured membranes. The amniotic fluid covers, insulates and protects against external infections. It was likely that the baby would be born prematurely, and even worse, with undeveloped lungs. Cord prolapse, deformed limbs, pulmonary hypoplasia – the list was long and the words scary. I was also at high risk of contracting an infection myself.

A garland of medical acronyms was being strung round my baby's neck. Each worse than the other. A risk of SCID. Now a new monster called PPROM.

A senior doctor joined the doctors and technicians standing around me. 'We would really advise you to consider a termination,' he said. 'You are at risk. If you contract an infection, it could be fatal. You have your own family, your own life. You need to think of yourself.'

But this was my self. This was everything to me! This was all I wanted, all I lived for.

'I am fine. I don't have an infection. I was given antibiotics.'

'You don't have an infection at the moment, but you can still develop one. You need to very careful. We really think you should consider the option of terminating.'

Lying on the scan table, with a damaged womb and a worried heart, a voice spoke to me with an irrational but loud, unmistakably clear message. 'The baby will be fine.' It came and went quickly, but I heard it, and I felt its strength. I heard it and it resonated with what my heart felt. Or was it perhaps the voice of my heart? My conviction that everything would be fine was resolute. That was all I needed.

'I will not terminate.'

My husband nodded in unison.

After losing a child, do you ever, can you ever, ever terminate the helpless, the unformed?

When the medics realised we were not going to listen to their sound advice, they called a more senior doctor. She arrived and explained the risks again. She talked about the chances of SCID recurring. 'You know how devastating that can be, having lost one child already.'

'That was because we lived in India and there was no treatment available. They treat it here in Great Ormond Street Hospital. I have friends with children who are completely cured,' I said, as if holding a trump card.

The doctor smiled, the sort of smile reserved for the doomed and the stubborn. 'OK, even though the risk is significant, we don't have to decide on a course of action today. You seem well and don't have a temperature. There is a very small amount of fluid around the baby. It's not enough, but there is a little bit. You are not in labour. We can decide on a termination depending on how things progress in the next few days.'

They fixed an appointment for the next week, telling me in the same breath that there was no chance I would be back because I would go into labour and push out a little fifteen week foetus.

The long report they printed out for us was gloomy, to say the least. I read it on the way home in the car. It stated that they were almost certain I was carrying a boy though I would need another scan in a few weeks to be sure. It ended by saying that the parents had been advised of the risks but were not willing to terminate. Needless to say, due to the rupture, any other invasive diagnostic tests were out of the question. I had been worrying about CVS and amniocentesis unnecessarily. My fate was to worry about something much bigger. Another unexpected challenge.

We called our parents in India. We heard the worry in their voices, but equally their strong support to hang on in there. We believed in a miracle, we told one other. Whatever was in store for us, we would accept it but we would not terminate a much awaited, much prayed for baby. I had pined, met doctors, consulted alternative healers, visited temples, read books of hope. Had it resulted in my conception? The baby's soul had come to us after a long wait, just when we were giving up, so we had to believe in a divine grace. Everything I had read about positive visualisation – *you are never given a wish without the power of making it true*[14] – told me that when I was given what I had asked for, I must not forsake it.

I spent the week at home. I joined a PPROM online support group. There was a section devoted to personal stories sequenced according to the week of the rupture. An entry in blue indicated that the baby had died and an entry in green indicated a live birth. Sometimes, if not always, the babies who had survived PPROM were premature and had to undergo several operations. These positive stories told of children who were alive, happy and healthy. I held on to those stories of hope, firmly ignoring the

---

14 Richard Bach: *You are never given a wish without the power of making it come true. You may have to work for it however*

voice of reason which pointed out a different fact. With the exception of two cases, the 'I ruptured in fourteen weeks stories' were all in blue.

Emails arrived from women all over the world. Those who had experienced success offered me advice about improving my chances, like minimising physical movement, taking complete bed rest and drinking cranberry juice to prevent infection. A few who had ruptured around the same time as me were worrying and meeting doctors and being told the same as I was told. Terminate, or if not, be prepared for a tragic outcome. We offered one another hope and shared details of our days. A day with no leakage was the best news. We shared information about our diets and how much water we drank. We were supposed to drink five to ten litres a day.

All day I sat up in bed with my laptop, trying to work. I went downstairs only once to the kitchen to heat my lunch in the microwave. In the evening, when my husband came back, I went downstairs for dinner but he made most of the trips to the kitchen to warm the food, clean up and so on. Then, I went back upstairs to bed.

I was due for another scan at King's. I was hopeful they would see a baby swimming in fluid. I had drunk litres of water and rested. There had been no more leaking.

After a long wait in the crowded waiting room, it was my turn. A locum doctor did the scan. The fluid level, or CPI index, was slightly higher than the previous week but still abysmally low. He knew our medical background, and pressing the probe, looking at the grainy picture on the screen, he nodded.

'Yes, it is a boy, for sure. Definitely.'

He stared at the picture for another moment and then said,

'You know, I can put in writing that this baby won't make it.

'But the fluid has increased a little. Isn't that positive?'

'That makes no difference! This pregnancy is just not possible!' He looked at us in disbelief.

We looked like rational, normal human beings but we were not listening to reason. I was so sure everything would be fine with every cell of my body telling me this is not what it seems. I looked at the fuzziness and made a promise to my baby, to the shadowy shape. 'Baby, you hold on, and I will hold on. I will do everything in my power, and more.' I ignored the doctor's words.

We were joined by the senior doctor, who had told us last time that we needn't take an immediate decision about a termination.

'You see, the baby has to keep producing fluid which is why amniotic fluid increases as the baby grows. It's only sixteen weeks. He is tiny. He won't be able to produce enough to raise the fluid to the required level. That is why we think this is not a viable pregnancy. Still, we are only doctors. There is a lot we don't know. We are not always right.'

I wanted to tell her that indeed they couldn't be right this time. There had to be something they could do.

'I am drinking a lot of water. I am on bed rest. Won't that make a difference?'

Once again, they gave me patient smiles, 'We don't advise you to change anything about your life. If it has to happen, it will. Drinking water and being on bed rest won't really help at this stage.'

My miracle baby will be fine, I wanted to tell them but could see that they would think I was completely irrational.

2

The following week, Mr. Smith did another scan. As he looked at the screen, his face was grim.

'Do you feel you are in labour?' he asked. I didn't think it was a sensible question but said nothing.

'No, I don't. I feel perfectly fine.'

Mr. Smith was talking to my husband. He went through the risks again prematurity and the tiny lungs being too rigid to work outside the womb. The fact that it was a boy meant a fifty percent chance he would have SCID. So many unknowns, so many question marks. Even Mr. Smith acknowledged that things were tough.

I tried to get up from the examining table but the room was swimming and my body floating. I slumped back down.

'Are you all right?' I heard anxious voices. I was lost. I had fainted.

'I am so sorry. I think I scared you.' Mr. Smith called a nurse who took my blood pressure.

'It's fine. I'm just overcome, I guess.'

I had fainted only a couple of times in my life. The first was when I stayed awake all night before an examination which was worrying me and then felt faint writing my paper. The second was when I was trying to take a flight from Delhi to Beirut via Dubai to attend a work meeting and missed my connections due to delays and fog in Delhi. At the airline desk, trying to find an alternate route and realising there was no way I could make the meeting in time, I fainted. None of those incidents came close to this one.

'Please don't worry. I will do my best for this baby,' Mr. Smith continued. 'I'm afraid we also need to consider the possibility of SCID, which is why it's so important neither of you get an infection. I've put you on low dose erythromycin as a prophylaxis. There is a little bit of fluid around the baby. We should remain vigilant, monitor you regularly and keep hoping the fluid levels will rise.'

'But King's is so negative. The doctor said he could put in writing that the baby won't make it. Can't I have my scans here? It takes the whole day to go there and sitting in the car for a few hours, there's more leaking.'

'Car travel won't bring on fluid leakage and you do need to go to King's for your scans. They have more sophisticated equipment and can check for abnormalities and deformities. But please don't get disheartened by what they say. It's their opinion. I will check your reports as well.'

'I will come back, meet you and feel better!' I joked.

We booked an appointment with him in two weeks. I was still injecting myself with Clexane every day and would continue throughout the pregnancy. Mr. Smith had stopped the pessaries after the PPROM because anything inserted wasn't recommended, but for years afterwards I would wonder if that was the cause of the infection and subsequent rupture. Could I have picked up an infection by not washing my hands adequately after my train and tube journeys? Mr. Smith said it was impossible to know the cause; the swab only showed which bacteria was present. I didn't ask further. I was scared he might tell me my own carelessness was indeed responsible.

We had confirmation we would have a boy. The question now was, if he survived PPROM, would he have SCID? I thought about all the times people had said it wouldn't happen again. 'God won't be so unkind,' they had said.

Years ago, I used to have frequent regular nightmares in which I dreamt about helpless babies. One dream stood out because it was so vivid. There was a very happy, shining little baby. He was giggling and laughing. My voice broke in mock despair. 'But you little baby, you have come out too early. I can't put you back inside me and now you are telling me you need a bone marrow transplant?' The happy baby had laughed even louder. Then I woke. What a vision. A joyful baby who decided to come out of the womb too early, complete with SCID.

3

I was still working from home but was increasingly worried about travelling to meetings.

'I need to go to Newbury and Reading and other places about for work. Is it safe to be running for trains?' I asked Dr. Patel.

'Bed rest won't stop the leakage. If it's going to happen, it will,' she said. 'Still, you are perfectly entitled to take some days off work.' She wrote me yet another sick note.

I told my boss that I had more serious health problems and he was not pleased. 'When do you think you can travel? For the moment, we can cover your meetings but there is a lot happening. We need to have you back.'

I wouldn't be able to commute until the end of the pregnancy and I did not know how long the pregnancy would last. It was too early to ask for maternity leave. 'I will know more after my next scan. I need to be careful for the next month or so,' I said as confidently as I could. The company was male-dominated, aggressive and the last place for a pregnant woman with ruptured membranes. My boss didn't push it. Perhaps he believed me, or perhaps he genuinely felt for me. He was English and it was ironic that none of the other colleagues, all men of Indian origin, were even remotely sympathetic. The bully boss was also Indian – a new age Indian perhaps.

The days passed. I drank a lot of cranberry juice. My husband had moved the microwave to the spare bedroom upstairs. Every morning, he left cereal, milk, a microwave ready meal from the local Waitrose, cutlery, juice and several bottles of water for me. All I had to do was walk the few steps from the bedroom to the spare room to get my food. I didn't have to cope with the stairs much.

A month passed. Scans in King's, blood tests in the local hospital, visits to Mr. Smith, the bin filling up with Clexane syringes, my stomach growing, the fluid levels rising. I was only eighteen weeks pregnant. At least another eighteen weeks to go if all went well. My husband worried all day about me on my own. Finally, he asked my parents if they would come and stay with us to give us support.

They arrived from India on a cold day in November, a shock since the previous time it had been summer and daylight until ten in the night. Now, the evenings were long, the rain heavy. Once they had to walk to the surgery to pick up a prescription for me. It was raining and so windy that the large umbrella flapped and they struggled to hold on to it. They were not used to this, having domestic help to cook and clean and run errands. It was all too much for them and too much of a contrast to the tropical country they had left! Much later I found out that prescriptions and medicines could be delivered to patients who weren't mobile. But we didn't know then so they went out on their daily errands. My husband took a day off every week to drive me to King's. He couldn't ask for more. His colleagues were being more considerate than mine.

I was a vessel, a vessel for a precious baby I had to hold on to and keep safe. My body had failed me three times so far – passing on a defective X chromosome to my first baby, developing endometriosis, and having a womb that was inhospitable for its precious cargo.

My mind fought with my body, willing it to hold on.

4

Sometimes I lay in bed, laptop to one side, looking up at the crack on the ceiling. We would have to repair it at some point, I would think.

One day, I heard a haunting tune on the radio. Israel Kamakawiwo'ole sang *Somewhere over the rainbow*. I wept silent tears. I wanted to see that rainbow. I wanted to believe.

I wrote long emails to women I didn't know but our exchanges were more intimate than those I would write to my best friends.

Three times a day my mother walked up the stairs, tray in hand, bearing meals. She cooked all day even though I'd never had much of an appetite. She planned my favourite childhood meals. Fish cutlets, fried aubergines, fried fish, prawn curry. She cooked with a passion, stirring her love into those meals. The smells reached me as I lay in bed resolutely injecting myself, drinking water and counting days. I drank a strong Korean brew of stewed roots which tasted terrible, bitter and smelly. My husband's boss insisted it would help, an age-old remedy in his native Korea. Every morning, my father brought up a glass of this concoction and five large bottles of water to drink throughout the day.

Each day was important. The baby grew stronger and closer to viability. You hold and I will hold. I repeated my promise to my baby like a mantra.

My husband returned in the evening with the Metro. Reading

it reminded me of the times I had run in and out of crowded trains. He would look at my face and know if I had a good day (no leaking) or a bad day.

We offered prayers every evening, some suggested by my mother, some by others we had met in Pondicherry. First I would recite the Hanuman Chalisa, a hymn to the God Hanuman, forty verses in Awadhi. The words were initially unfamiliar, a different language on my tongue, but gradually I learnt to recite the ancient words. Hanuman is the God who helps you face obstacles and hardship or bhigna in life. The words calmed and soothed me. Then I would read one page from the book *Savitri* by Sri Aurobindo about overcoming death. With her intelligence and love, Savitri outwitted Yama, the God of death who had to bring her husband, Satyavan, back to life. My mother read one page of the Gita aloud the discourse Lord Krishna gave to Arjuna on the battlefield of Kurukshetra, a tale of fate, life, destiny, conquering and fighting. All these prayers should help me to remain positive, to believe in the impossible, and to make my body believe in it as well. Maybe the baby inside heard and imbibed the wise words.

Prayer time became part of the fabric of my life.

I chanted the '*Maha Mrutyunjaya mantra*' over and over when I couldn't sleep, when I waited for a scan, when I wanted to feel my baby's kicks. It was a prayer to Lord Shiva in unfamiliar Sanskrit which became second nature to me. It would remain so over the years, for always.

Om Tryambakam Yajamahe
Sugandhim Pushtivardhanam
Urvarukamiva Bandhanan
Mrityor Mukshiya Maamritat

Meaning:

We meditate on the three-eyed reality
Which permeates and nourishes all like a fragrance.
May we be liberated from death for the sake of immortality,
Even as the cucumber is severed from bondage to the creeper

A cab arrived twice a week to take us to the local hospital for a blood test and a scan. I didn't drive anymore, nor did anyone want me to go anywhere on my own. Every second, every minute, was fear ridden. What if something happens?

One Saturday evening, my husband and parents asked me if I could come downstairs for dinner, to join them just for once instead of eating alone in bed.

'Nothing will go wrong,' he said. 'It's only ten to twelve steps.'

I agreed, my parents looked delighted, but with each step, I worried. Sitting at the dining table felt unreal. Should I be sitting on a hard chair? Could it start the leakage again? I missed my huddled self on the bed, eating my food from a tray, on my own. Talking with everyone, enjoying our meal, appreciating the food, everything felt superficial. I ate quickly and told them I wanted to go back to bed. They looked crestfallen. They had thought maybe I could watch a movie with them, relax a little. I ignored their looks and went upstairs.

Safely back in my duvet I wondered if I was the same person. The same person who had flown to Africa at the drop of a hat to attend a work meeting? Who thought nothing of going to Ghana to negotiate contracts and on the way back, stopping in Amsterdam to meet friends and then flying out from London the next day to Sweden? Could I ever become that person again?

All I wanted to do was to lie still, keep my baby safe, talk to the doctors and email other mums. Nothing else mattered to me.

I caught a bad cold and cough. Every time I coughed, my stomach hurt and I worried the fluid would leak. I called Mr. Smith on his mobile to tell him, and just hearing his voice reassured me. I longed for my next appointment.

Lying on the bed, I had enough time to worry about the future and think about the past. I remembered one event in particular when I'd visited a shrine under a tree in Calcutta. It was when my first baby boy was unwell and Suchitra, the nanny, had insisted that prayers to this goddess were all we needed to make him well. One evening, with Suchitra and other women from the slum opposite us, my baby in my arms, we walked to the tree. It was already dusk and the lights on the narrow road were dim. They were all mothers and they felt for me. They were sure their devi would help me and cure my son. How could I possibly explain the science of genetics and faulty chromosomes to them? I couldn't explain that nothing could be done for him in his country of birth. I knew all that, yet I prostrated myself before the dark-eyed goddess, like the other women, knowing that the prayer wouldn't work, yet praying with them. That evening, Suchitra had sung a bit louder, a lot happier, convinced her babushuna would be well.

Now, thinking about the two conditions – SCID and pulmonary hypoplasia (lung failure due to PPROM) – I drew a grid with all the possible options. I felt calmer with it written in black and white. It was something like this:

	SCID	No SCID
No Pulmonary Hypoplasia	Curable after a bone marrow transplant	Miracle ☺
Pulmonary Hypoplasia	Worst outcome, no possibility of survival	Not relevant since no possibility of survival, so SCID makes no difference

I concentrated on the top right quadrant, telling myself the more I focused on it, the more I would influence the result. The outcome had to be a miracle.

I read about a procedure called an amnio-patch which was used to repair a tear in the womb, rather like a Band-Aid over a cut. It was carried out mostly in America, not in the UK and Europe. My mother researched further and found the name of a doctor in America who had successfully used it. Somebody in my support group knew him and sent me his address. An email didn't hurt. So I emailed Dr. O'Brien and very soon, he was emailing me almost every other day.

Dr. O'Brien told me straightaway that he couldn't offer his treatment to me because he only tried to patch ruptures resulting from an invasive prenatal diagnostic test, like an amnio or CVS. Since the cause of my rupture was unknown or attributed to an infection, I wouldn't be a good case. Yet he took the trouble to answer my every email and my every question. It wasn't that I doubted Mr. Smith, but since treatment protocols varied in the US and UK, I wanted to find out all I could. I needed to be in a position of having as much information as possible so that I could question my doctors if I had doubts. My emails to Dr. O'Brien lasted from November till January. Years later, I would come across the email trail, a long list of questions and anxiety, and his responding support and encouragement.

As always, the internet, the constant communication with complete strangers, the hope and the goodwill I received from people I had never seen, nor would ever see, shaped my days. That interaction helped me survive.

Behind every door I had knocked on, from those days in Calcutta when we were trying to raise funds for treatment till now, there had been an answer, help and support.

5

The weeks passed by. The less eventful the day, the better. Once a week I had a scan at the local hospital and every two weeks at King's to measure the Average Fluid Index (AFI). It was the most crucial measurement. I remembered each number and willed it to climb higher. A week after the rupture the AFI was 1.2 cms, three weeks later 1.8 cms, and five weeks after that 3.2 cms. Normal values ranged from 8-18 cms at nineteen weeks. Perhaps more significantly, the deepest pool of liquid measured 2 cms. The scans showed the small pools and with utter delight I saw my baby's face lying in one of the deepest ones.

It was December, and I was close to twenty-four weeks, the first step to viability. This was a significant milestone, the time we had been waiting for. If the worst happened and I went into labour, the medical world would make a huge effort to save my baby. I was getting close to bringing my baby ashore. Only a few more days.

In America, the protocol was hospitalisation and complete bed rest once you reached this point of viability. Strictly sticking to this with not even shower or restroom breaks, you had the best chance of avoiding preterm labour. One of the worrying possibilities was placental abruption – a breaking away of the placenta because of a lack of fluid. Another was cord prolapse when the umbilical cord can fall into the birth canal. Both of these were high-risk emergencies. If either happened, one would be rushed to hospital in an ambulance, in fact the window for delivering the baby was only five to ten minutes. After that, death was inevitable. If I was already in hospital, such an emergency would be treated promptly and while the baby would be extremely premature at twenty-four weeks, at least a fatality might be avoided.

But in England there were different practices. Doctors regarded hospitalisation as a poor choice because of the risk of hospital infections. We lived close enough to the hospital to make it in a few minutes. They told me to stay alert and to come immediately if I spiked a temperature, started bleeding or experienced a sudden increase in fluid leakage. I wondered if the differences in protocol were due to the medical care systems, privatised and fee-paying in America, government-funded in England.

With Christmas not far away, I was getting increasingly anxious. I asked the nurse who was taking my bloods what would happen if something went wrong during the holidays?

'The hospital is always open,' she said. 'You can always come here if you need to.'

Still I worried. I wouldn't be able to see Dr. Patel or Mr. Smith. My lifelines would not be available during the festive period. Of course I could go to A&E but that wasn't very reassuring.

The fluid loss and I had settled into an acceptable pattern. I passed most days without any apparent leakage. Sometimes I would see a small discharge in the toilet but I reasoned it away. A feminine discharge. Or because my pelvic muscles weren't strong enough and I strained when coughing. Or my eyes played a trick and there was nothing there. Sometimes I asked my mother for a second opinion. Once, she looked at the liquid I had wiped on to some toilet roll and said it was fluid. I panicked. In the evening when my husband returned, he knew from the expression on my face that I was worrying.

In a state of constant anxiety, I carried on until the week before Christmas when on the 19th of December, there was a clear warning sign. I started bleeding in the middle of the night. My husband rushed me to the hospital. I was strapped to a machine to check uterine contractions and if I was going into labour. The nurses left me and carried on with their other chores. I watched the spidery lines on the screen, listened to the duk-duk-duk-duk of my baby's heartbeat. The readings were normal, meaning I wasn't in labour. Still they said they would have to keep me under observation for at least forty-eight hours so I would be there for the night. I would be discharged if I remained stable. They also decided that this was a good time to give me one of the two recommended steroid shots. Steroid injections helped the baby's lungs to grow. In cases of PPROM, one was usually given at twenty-four weeks, and the second just before the baby was due. To have reached this milestone of being eligible for a steroid shot was a big event. The nurse swiftly plunged the needle into my leg and I prayed for the steroids to reach my baby's lungs and do their job.

They also gave me my Clexane shot. There wasn't much space left on my stomach which was mottled and bruised from self-injecting so they inserted the needle into my leg – much harder to do yourself.

Visiting hours were twice a day, for two hours. My husband and parents were due in the morning. I was taken to the maternity ward and allocated a corner bed close to the window. There were three other women, each in a cubicle, curtained off for privacy. I would later find the nurses insisted the curtains were pulled wide open every morning so we had to face each other, face the world. If we wanted to, we could draw them closed at bedtime. All three women looked very pregnant, ready to deliver. The one opposite me looked settled and relaxed as she watched the little television set over the bed. I desperately wanted to be back home, united with my laptop.

I hardly slept that night. The ward was noisy and all night I could hear the rattle of nurses rushing past, babies crying in other wards. There were no babies in my ward and the others, like me, were struggling through their pregnancy. I talked to the woman opposite when we met in the bathroom. She was eight months pregnant and had a low-lying placenta so was on bed rest and in hospital long term which is why she looked so settled. My own story sounded unbelievable – waters breaking at fourteen weeks, loss of my first child. I behaved like an imposter, as if I too was a first-time mum and as clueless as the other young mums. It was interesting to see which conditions were prescribed bed rest while some, like mine had no treatment plan.

PPROM was like an orphan disease, no one wanted to own and invest in.

The hospital had its own routine. Breakfast, lunch and dinner trays were brought to the corridor outside. Breakfast was always white toast and tea, lunch served early at noon and dinner around five in the evening. It was too early for me and the meals were insipid. We had to walk along the long corridor to get our plates and then leave them in another corner. This was more walking than I had done for months. The toilets were at the end of another long corridor. I worried about all that walking.

I had a box of antiseptic wipes and diligently wiped the toilet every time I used it. I had to do my best. My body, my mind, my heart had to work in unison to carry this baby as best as I could.

I had a routine outpatient appointment booked with Mr. Smith for the following day. I asked the nurse if I could still go, even though I was in hospital. She mumbled about not being allowed across to the outpatients side until I was discharged, and they could only discharge me after the forty-eight-hours, even though there had been no bleeding, not a spot. She seemed surprised that I wanted to meet Mr. Smith when I was in hospital and being looked after. I felt desperate and must have looked it because she eventually agreed to ask the doctors on duty for permission.

Mr. Smith also did ward duty, but unfortunately it wasn't his turn this month. The doctor on duty was his counterpart, and perhaps his competitor in some sense with possibly some peer rivalry because she didn't seem pleased with my demand for Mr. Smith.

'Mr. Smith has put me on erythromycin, so I shall have it.'

'Mr. Smith has advised heparin injections throughout the pregnancy so I must have it.'

She made a few comments about checking my records and deciding what was best to do in the circumstances but I kept repeating like a parrot, 'Can I see Mr. Smith tomorrow in the out-patients?'

The day passed without incident. The next morning, the nurse told me I could go to outpatients and see Mr. Smith. Depending on what he said, I could be discharged that evening.

My parents arrived at visiting hours as always. They were by now used to periods of solitude and waiting in hospitals. They had each brought a book and sat at the foot of my bed, reading. I felt relief as my appointment got closer. It would be a bit of a walk. The hospital was new and spread over several buildings with wards at the end of the corridors, adding further extension, but the reassurance I would receive from Mr. Smith would see me through. We planned to walk slowly so we needed to leave almost thirty minutes before the appointment and I made sure I went to the toilet before setting off on what was, for me, a long trip.

What happened next was almost as shocking as the gush of fluid I had experienced at fourteen weeks five days.

When I stood up, it felt as if something had exploded inside and the water in the toilet was red. Bright red. I stared and stared in horror. All the acronyms, always in my mind, like the planets circling the sun, shouted their names loudly. I was still not twenty-four weeks. I had a long way to go. If this massive bleed was from a placental abruption, the baby had little hope.

I stared as if maybe it could all be washed away, as if by looking long enough the blood could find its way back into my body. Then I flushed it and walked back to the ward, shaking, wondering if I was leaving a trail of blood behind me.

My parents were sitting in the same position. I got into bed. I looked at them.

'Should we leave now?' my mother asked.

I had to tell them. I knew there would be terrible worry on both of their faces. My father was a heart patient. He really didn't need shocks as well as working so hard at home to look after me. I wanted to insulate them from everything happening, but I was lost myself. And very scared.

'I just had some more bleeding….it was …well, huge. A lot.'

'A lot? How do you mean…how much? What happened?'

I was too shaken to describe it again.

'We need to call someone!' My father pressed the buzzer at my bedside.

'Extreme bleeding. It was scary. A lot of blood,' I mumbled to the nurse when she came. She took one look at me.

'OK, let's get you all settled and relaxed and we'll call the doctor. Let's just see what's happening.' She strapped me to the machine that measured contractions.

I saw the familiar lines, the comforting duk-duk-duk-duk. The nurse said it looked fine, no contractions, no stressed baby.

I called my husband and asked him to go straight to Mr. Smith's clinic on his own because I wasn't allowed out and anyway I didn't want to risk walking. Yet I wanted to know what Mr. Smith had to say about the latest big bleed. My husband joked about being the only man meeting a gynaecologist on his own, and set off for gynae outpatients.

The doctor on duty, a middle-aged man, arrived soon. He said he would need to do an internal examination. I yelled from my horizontal position that he wasn't supposed to do that, that I was a patient with a high risk of infection. I knew that Mr. Smith would rule out anything that was a potential risk.

So he didn't do an internal examination. I lay down, legs spread, bent at the knee while he just looked, 'You are dilated almost 1.5 centimeters,' he said. 'We have to send you to a hospital which can look after preemies.' He left abruptly to make calls to find a suitable place for me.

'But I am not dilated. I can't be!' I said to everyone around me.

My parents looked stricken. We all knew the maths. Every day counted. Twenty-four weeks was the first point of viability. There was a big difference between a baby below the gestational age of twenty-four weeks and even a day above. If I was really dilated and ready to give birth, my baby would be born at twenty-three weeks and this would mean he would have a tough struggle. Girls were typically stronger than boys at birth and once again I thought, had this been a girl, the risk wouldn't have been so great.

My husband arrived after an hour, smiling, thanks to Mr. Smith giving him some hope. 'It's nothing to worry about. Mr. Smith said it's your placenta moving or something. He will come and see you after his clinic.'

My placenta was indeed lying a bit low. They had confirmed this in previous scans, not low enough to be a medical condition like the woman in my ward, but low enough to have been noted. Mr. Smith had said it was nothing to worry about and at some point in the pregnancy it would surely move upwards but he hadn't said anything about simultaneous bleeding. Still, I was relieved. I needed his opinion. I refused to believe I was dilating until he told me I was.

The doctor who had gone to find me another hospital came back jubilantly.

'We have found you a bed in Queen Charlotte hospital in Hammersmith. They have a very good neonatal unit. Here we only manage babies from twenty-eight weeks whereas they care for babies from twenty-four weeks. We will call an ambulance and you'll be taken there.' He looked like he had achieved a major victory, and possibly he had in the busy NHS world where beds were hard to find. But this news wasn't welcome, to put it mildly.

Hammersmith in west London was at the opposite end of town. How were my parents supposed to visit me? They couldn't commute by train or tube on their own. They said they could but with their health conditions, we didn't want them to. How many days would I have to stay there?

There was no sign of Mr. Smith. I was getting worried that he'd forgotten and wouldn't come, and I would be sent off in an ambulance. He turned up at six in the evening, two hours later than he had promised. He spoke to the nurses and checked the reports.

'You aren't in labour at all. It's your placenta moving. You had a low-lying placenta which can move at this time of the pregnancy. I had told you it would,' he said, without examining me further.

'But there was a lot of blood.'

'Yes, there would be but that doesn't mean anything. It's only the placenta moving.'

I thought about what the nurse had said, that a drop of blood can colour a glass of water and it always looks more than there really is.

'But the doctor is sending me to Hammersmith which is too far for us!'

'You are lucky it's only Hammersmith. Sometimes people are sent as far as Bristol. They are airlifted when in labour.'

'But you said I am not in labour!' The machine hadn't picked up any contractions, so all I had was the doctor's word.

'You are not in labour. But isn't it best for the baby? What if something does happen tomorrow? Wouldn't it be better to be in a hospital which can look after younger babies? Our facilities are only for babies above twenty-eight weeks. We must always choose what is best for the baby.'

He had a point. Hammersmith wasn't that far. It was still London. My husband said he could come every day after work. He worked in the city. My parents wouldn't be able to see me every day but they could visit over the weekend with my husband. During the Christmas holidays, he would be home.

Mr. Smith wished me good luck and left. I was out of his care for now. I felt I was on my own.

From my bed, I watched him talking to my parents. I saw him take my mother's hands in his, saw her with head bent over his hands. Later I would ask her what that was about and she would confess sheepishly she had broken down and told him they were so worried about me. He had promised that he would do his best. 'We are all with her. She will be fine,' he had told her as she wept.

People speak of the English as cold and stiff. That gesture from the smartly dressed, calm doctor was a defining moment for me and my relationship with this country I had chosen as home.

6

Visiting hours were coming to an end and my ambulance still hadn't arrived. My husband had gone home, dropped my parents and come back with a haphazardly packed suitcase. My mother had sent all my prayer books. There could be no disruption in my routine.

I had practically no maternity clothes. Since every day could have been the last day of my pregnancy, it had seemed pointless buying anything. I had spent my days at home in loose tops and trousers and I had a couple of going-to-the-hospital outfits. I had never felt so dumpy in my life yet the friends who cared enough to visit me commented on how beautiful I looked and how glowing.

The ambulance eventually arrived late in the evening. I wasn't a very urgent case and didn't need the screaming blue lights. I was only being taken in an ambulance, in case I needed any attention or care on the way.

One of my good friends lived in Hammersmith, quite close to Queen Charlotte. I messaged them and they promised to come and see me in the hospital at whatever time we got there. They were away on holiday over the Christmas period and offered to leave their flat keys with us so my parents could spend time there between visiting hours at the weekend. Help was always there. I was blessed in that sense. Wherever I knocked, there was someone to listen. Sometimes I didn't even have to knock and a friend or kind stranger was there to help or sympathise. I never felt let down by the system or the doctors treating me.

Who would have thought that one day I would be driven across London in an ambulance, lying on a stretcher, in the back! All I could see through the windows were the street lights dipping in and out. It always took a while to get from the south east to the west of London through the evening traffic but when you are lying on a narrow bed in a moving vehicle and can only guess where you are, it seems a lot longer.

'Have we crossed the river yet?' I asked my husband, trying to imagine the London Eye, Big Ben, all the sights of the city I loved and lived in.

I saw some familiar grey stone buildings. 'Are we in the city?'

'Was that Brixton now?' as graffiti whizzed past.

It took an hour and a half to reach Queen Charlotte and then the sense of urgency was palpable. After the quiet, restful journey when I sometimes drifted off to sleep, the voices sounded unnecessarily loud. People gathered round the ambulance doors. I was wheeled out and taken to a large empty room.

'Is there any chance she could get something to eat?' my husband asked, as they were strapping me to the machine to check for contractions. We were both starving. I had missed dinner and he'd had no time to eat either.

'Dinner has already been served here. It's too late now. Maybe we can find you a sandwich,' the nurse said.

An older, possibly more senior nurse came in, took one look at my face, and said, 'But you are not in labour.'

'I should hope not,' I said. 'I don't want to be in labour.'

'But we were told a twenty-three weeker in labour was arriving.

You certainly are not and after all these years, would I know if someone is in labour or not!' she laughed.

I felt relieved. Maybe they would now realise it was all a mistake and let us go.

A doctor arrived. Once again, I put my legs up, bent my knees. Several medics stood at the bottom of the bed and looked between my legs.

'Did they do an internal examination in Farnborough?' the doctor asked.

'No. They aren't meant to because my membranes are ruptured.'

'So why did he think you were dilated?'

'I don't know. He just sort of looked and told me I'm 1.5 cms dilated. Then they sent me here.'

'The doctors in Farnborough must eat a lot of carrots then,' he said. 'I can't see anything, let alone dilation, given the amount of fluid and blood in the opening.'

When I described this later, my father was tickled pink and laughed at the carrot statement for weeks. At that moment, however, I caught on to the other part of his sentence.

'Fluid? I am not leaking any more.'

'Actually you are. There is a lot of fluid there. But no dilation.'

That was a scary observation because I hadn't felt any leakage. Had I been leaking all along without my knowledge? Would my baby's lungs develop?

We assumed we would be allowed to go home since birth wasn't imminent but the doctor said we would need to stay now that I was here until they were sure there was no further risk or until twenty-eight weeks. Whichever happened first. It was 23rd December. I was going to spend Christmas in hospital.

My friends visited with books. A nurse brought me a sandwich. My husband went home on the train, an hour and half journey, and planned his trip back the next day.

7

The ward they took me to was quiet. Clean, light blue plush carpets. Four beds in one ward, surrounded by curtains which actually went all the way, forming a little room. It was like a private hospital. One of the other patients, a tall blonde girl, was still awake, her curtains open. She smiled a shy, welcoming smile.

It was late and I was tired but the hospital didn't sleep. Several people came to see me including a nurse from the neonatal unit. She wanted to show me the unit so that I would be prepared. I said I would rather wait and go with my husband, since I didn't need to see it in the middle of the night. When she realised I was determined not to go, she told me a little about the care they offered and left me to rest.

I plodded to the bathroom, my movements so much slower with my big belly. Given the lack of fluid, my stomach was strangely swollen. The bathroom was much closer than in Farnborough and it was a relief to walk less.

The morning held another pleasant surprise. Breakfast arrived on the ward and you could even choose your jam, and ask for a coffee or tea. They also took lunch and dinner orders. In terms of comfort, there was no choosing between the two hospitals. My parents and husband came later in the day. It was a long drive back and forth. It was also strange for them to be in my house without me. They had nobody to look after now.

And then it was Christmas! Much to our surprise, a Father Christmas visited us in the ward and gave us gifts. I got a rather useful mini-manicure set. The friendly girl in the opposite bed had her family coming for the Christmas lunch. She was only five months pregnant but had severe pre-eclampsia which had been diagnosed just before she was due to go on holiday. Pre-eclampsia is a pretty well-known condition but quite dangerous for both mother and child. The mother's blood pressure can rise high enough to damage vital organs and then the baby has to be delivered prematurely. Every day counted. In spite of the anxiety, the ward felt fairly festive. The other two beds remained empty

On New Year's Eve, I dared to walk to the TV room which was a whole corridor away to watch the fireworks over the London Eye. Last year I had been out there, in the cold, with friends, with lots of wine, as the world celebrated a new year. Here in the ward, as London's skies lit up, we wished one another a happy New Year. I started to walk back to my bed. What a relief to be back resting! It was hard now to imagine my past when I rushed from home to stations to office and back and then to the gym, out for a drink and dinner. It felt like a distant part of me. I didn't know what the next year would bring.

I continued with my prayer routine, now doing my mother's share of reading a page of the Gita as well.

Friends visited with books, with wishes, not knowing many of the details, expecting that very soon I would be home. I didn't tell them about all the things which could still go wrong, all the potential problems the doctors talked about and which stood in my brain like sentinels.

8

In hospital, I had no access to the internet. This was before the days of rampant Wi-Fi. It was good in a way because I couldn't follow the news in my support group and I couldn't search endlessly for information about my baby's development. I told my mother to check my emails and keep me informed of what was happening to my friends. I couldn't live a day without being in touch. I needed to know how they all were.

One weekend, I asked my mother about the PPROM group. She hemmed and hawed. She said she couldn't remember what had happened to M or R who, like me, were twenty-four weeks pregnant. She said people hadn't written in. She asked my father if he could remember but he didn't say much either. It was only when I was back at home that I understood their vagueness. None of the women who had ruptured membranes at the same time as me were still pregnant. Their stories had joined the list in blue.

While Queen Charlotte was much more comfortable than my local hospital, there was one problem. Doctors being doctors don't agree on treatment protocols and have different viewpoints. I was still having the erythromycin prescribed by Mr. Smith but the doctor on duty in Queen Charlotte did not agree with the treatment. 'We need to stop the erythromycin. You can't be on long-term antibiotics because it will mask any infection you may get. You could have an infection without us knowing. The bacteria can also become resistant to the antibiotic so we won't be able to treat you.'

'But if I do get an infection, then the baby will need to be delivered and it's still so early.'

'Yes, that's a risk we have to take. We can deal with it if it happens. I would rather deal with that than an infection we can't control.'

I could see the sense in his argument but my focus was on having my baby inside for as long as possible. I didn't agree with his ideas, thinking it was a matter of life or death for my baby. The next morning, I called Mr. Smith. He had given me his mobile number, my personal helpline. 'What would you have done? Would you still prescribe antibiotics?'

'Yes, because that gives your baby the best chance. They need to regularly check your temperature and have blood tests twice a week to check whether you have an infection. The CRP and WBC levels will tell them if you have caught something.'

'But what if I become resistant to the antibiotic?'

'There are many more to choose from,' he said. 'You're on a low dose of erythromycin. It helps in this kind of a situation.' I knew that everyone in the support group had been prescribed antibiotics, but for a few weeks, not throughout the pregnancy. What Mr. Smith was suggesting seemed controversial. 'Another reason to keep you on an antibiotic is that in a hospital you are exposed to more germs.'

Who should I trust? The doctor who had brought me successfully to this stage, or the doctors in the hospital who were all following the tried and tested approach? The doctor who foolishly believed, like me, that miracles could happen or the doctors who believed that science was always right? I felt sure there was an unseen force, a grace which was working for me and my baby. I wrote to Dr. O Brien for another opinion. He wasn't too concerned about the antibiotics though he thought they should be stopped at twenty-eight weeks. He said since I was only being treated with one antibiotic, and not three or four, I should be safe. If I became resistant to one antibiotic, there were others. His opinion was similar to that of Mr. Smith.

I had a little stash of erythromycin from the previous prescription but it would run out in a week. Since it now looked as if I would stay here till I was twenty-eight weeks at least, we had to think of something. Mr. Smith couldn't write me a prescription because I was under the care of Queen Charlotte.

At times like this, you think of other places where people can buy antibiotics without prescriptions as over the counter drugs or where medicines are cheap and easy to procure. You think of who might be travelling to London from India in the next few days or who might agree to post you a supply of antibiotics. We did both. One of my friends was in India on a business trip. He was a good enough friend to not probe much and didn't even ask why we needed the drugs. He bought a month's supply of erythromycin and brought it to me in hospital. My mother had also asked one of her friends in India to post us some. I had enough stock.

Meanwhile, my sister said her colleagues were incredulous and were asking what was wrong with the London doctors. Why had they allowed me to continue with such a high-risk pregnancy? It wouldn't be allowed in India.

'Don't they understand that there's a huge risk the child may not be normal?? What will you do then?' she asked me.

'Whatever happens, we will accept it. It's not for us to spurn this life we have been given. Until this soul himself wants to go, until then, we will do our best.'

My promise. You hold and I will hold, madly, stubbornly, in faith, in prayer.

There were prayers from India. One of my mother's acquaintances, Kamal Bhai, asked me to call him. He would then pray and send his blessings. Sometimes he asked for my husband as well who rolled his eyes in disbelief! We would have to sit quietly with our hands on our heads, while Kamal Bhai chanted at the other end of the phone. Under normal circumstances, I would find it hilarious. I was in a way used to this routine because he had done it before when I was trying to conceive. He had told me I would have a boy and that all would be well. I suspected he understood nothing about risks of ruptured membranes and possibly thought I was just unduly worried. Still I listened to him and appreciated his prayers

A part of me – the educated me who had studied Science and Engineering – said I was being really silly believing in people offering prayers who might well be charlatans. And another part of me, who believed in the beyond, and in what the eyes couldn't see, said I was right to accept good wishes and grace.

I still carried my antiseptic wipes with me to the bathroom. I cleaned the shower handles even. Next to my bed sat packs of cranberry juice. I didn't have the five bottles of water my father used to bring or the Korean brew, but I tried to drink as much water as I could. The food was better than in the other hospital. Still I waited for the weekend when my mother would bring fish cutlets or Indian sweets.

My fluid levels were rising. The index was now close to normal and the deepest pool more than two centimetres. According to Dr. O'Brien, the deepest pool was even more important than the fluid index. Some pools couldn't be measured as they were small or too close to the baby so it meant that if you added all the pockets together, the fluid level was actually higher than the measure on the index. Dr. Bhasin, the senior doctor on the ward, felt confident enough to tell me there was no risk of pulmonary hypoplasia because lung development starts around eighteen weeks and continues till about twenty-six, and during this time I had some deep pockets of fluid. He did say there still might be underlying lung issues but not rigid lungs unable to take in air. From the scans, everything else looked normal. There was a risk of the extremities being bent from the dry womb which would need corrective surgery at birth, but the scans indicated perfectly shaped feet and hands.

'Whatever condition you are in, you are mine,' I told my baby, whose form was sometimes visible, outlined faintly below my stomach. I remembered the last time, at term, I would feel the head distinctly, sometimes a foot, some really strong kicks.

The two pregnancies were worlds apart.

'Last time, the process was perfect, but the product flawed. This time, while the process has been flawed, the product has to be fine,' my sister-in-law said one day on the phone. The logic was sensible. When things have gone wrong once, by rights they shouldn't go wrong again. The universe, God, couldn't be so unjust.

But my philosophy, read and thought about, was different. God wasn't there to ensure everyone's life was easy and simple. God wasn't there to make sure that everyone's life progressed in the way we wanted. It was all down to the soul. The soul chooses its path before birth. The challenges and tribulations in life are chosen by the soul on its journey. There was always help on the way, if we prayed, if we believed. With this philosophy, I found it easier to accept my first baby's helplessness and death. With the soul of a saint, he chose a short, painful life and he chose me as his mother because he knew I could bear the grief and treasure him for my whole life. My second baby had the soul of a fighter and he chose me because I would be able to deal with the struggle and was determined to see it to the end. As for me, why had my soul chosen such a path? Who knew? Maybe the quest I sought was to become a mother, to feel a mother in every cell of my body, consciously and unconsciously. After all, you treasure and value something you have truly worked hard to achieve. Motherhood was something many women received easily and some took it casually. How many had had to really try to become a mother? And as you aspire and dream and work towards that realisation, your soul and your mind become more discerning and more intense.

9

A constant stream of pregnant women came, delivered their babies and left the ward. Only me and the friendly girl in the corner bed with pre-eclampsia stayed, hanging on to every day. Every extra day the baby stays inside the womb counted for both of us.

From our beds, we watched the others. A couple came in, the woman breathing loudly, pacing the room in pain, the man supporting her. We named them the Breather and the Hugger. 'They are nowhere near labour pains,' my mother said. Indeed, they were sent home to wait some more. A young Asian woman came in muttering quietly, perhaps chanting. It was her third and she paced quickly in short steps until they announced it was time for her to deliver. She was in and out of the hospital in a few hours, with her baby.

It was difficult to be with these mothers who were in pain but jubilant at the prospect of a little baby. We had no idea if this day would ever come and if it did, if things would be normal. We knew the possibility of a premature baby was very high for both of us. But there was nowhere else to place women like us, pregnant but with long-term complications.

By now, colleagues at work were getting more and more impatient. They couldn't carry on like this, they said. Either I had to start travelling and attending meetings or take time off indefinitely. They were hoping I would resign but I did no such thing. I asked for maternity leave and they had to accept it. Not one colleague visited me nor asked how I was. Unlike my previous organisation who had sent flowers after my operation, this company believed in letting the weak fall by the wayside.

For me, it was more relaxing to be on maternity leave and to not have to think about work for a whole year. At least I hoped it would be a year because I had only prayers for the outcome of the pregnancy.

My routine was steady, my day set in its predictability. I clung to that familiarity. I stayed in bed, I read. I prayed. I drank a lot of water. I chose my breakfast carefully. Toast today, cereal the next day, eggs cooked different ways. Lunch would be chicken soup tomorrow. A special treat for dinner – rice pudding for dessert, bringing back memories of the rich kheer of home. After breakfast, there was the nurse's visit and a blood pressure check. Sometimes it would be my turn to be strapped up on the machine and I'd have a blissful hour of hearing my baby's heartbeat. I loved those times of peace and sometimes the busy nurses didn't come back on time so I was left strapped on for much longer. Just my baby's duk-duk-duk-duk and me.

Dr. Bhasin came twice a week, before nine. The curtain around my bed would rustle and the team would say, 'Good morning.' I would sit up in bed. I loved meeting the doctors, loved to discuss what was wrong or right. My problem was their problem too. We were like family. Once the morning visits were over, I would walk slowly to the shower. Then a long phone call to my mother, then lunch, a nap, read, pray, wait for my husband in the evening, dinner, nurse visit, Clexane injection, read, sleep.

I had never rested so much in my life, nor focussed on one single outcome – having a healthy baby as close to term as possible.

10

We were taken on a tour of the neonatal centre. Tiny babies, so tiny that doll's clothes would be massive on them, were hooked up to gigantic machines with tubes and wires criss-crossing their incubators. A little baby at twenty-three weeks, too small even for the incubators, was placed in a little plastic bag. All around us, there was life. And people. Doctors and nurses, dedicated beyond measure, were out to save these tiny precious souls who had come too soon into the world. If it did happen that my baby was born too early, he would be safe here. They would do their best to save him. I went back to my bed reassured.

They took the other girl for a tour a few days later and she came back in tears because she was worried she might have a 'rat baby' who would have to fight every minute of her life. She had a point, of course, but my perspective was very different. With my first child, I too would have felt like that but now it was all about protecting and preserving what I had been granted. I explained to her that while it would be incredibly hard to see her baby go through something like that, the centre was proof of tremendous hope. I hadn't told her about my baby before. She only knew about my ruptured membranes and thought I was very brave and very calm.

It happened sooner for her. One night she was taken to the

labour room – she had been taken several times before and brought back – but this time she stayed. Her baby girl was born at twenty-eight weeks, weighing just about a kilo. She would grow up to be a beautiful, healthy child.

I was inching toward twenty-eight weeks. I had surprised the doctors here as well by holding strong. I mentioned the specialist scans I had been given in King's. They said I could be sent to King's in an ambulance but King's replied that I didn't need specialist scans any more and had been discharged from their outpatient ward. I should be monitored locally, they said. It meant my pregnancy was nearing some semblance of normality.

I called Mr. Smith to keep him updated. I told him that I was continuing with the erythromycin without going into the details and the subterfuge. Maybe he didn't want to know or maybe he guessed and decided to say nothing, thus becoming my accomplice. Now that we seemed to have reached the point of viability, he wanted to establish the protocol to manage the baby when he was born, in case he had SCID. He made a call to Dr. Patel, who got in touch with Guy's hospital, who got in touch with Great Ormond Street Hospital. Very soon, a letter came from Great Ormond addressed to the surgery, the midwife and myself, explaining what would happen when my baby was born.

We would need to be in a single room, in isolation. Right after birth, they would take a sample of the baby's blood. If possible, they would also preserve his cord blood for testing. The baby would be given anti-fungal drops immediately after birth. This was prophylactic. A precaution. The results should be back in a few hours but until that time, the baby would be treated as if he tested positive for SCID. There would be a protocol of hand washing by all staff handling the baby.

This was a milestone because here we were thinking in terms of the baby being viable.

11

I made it to twenty-eight weeks. Queen Charlotte didn't seem to be in a hurry to let me go and I had to ask the doctor a couple of times if I could. I had made many friends and the hospital was comfortable but my husband was commuting long journeys there and back. My parents had left the comfort of their own home to be with me and nurse me but I wasn't at home. I knew that Queen Charlotte would send me back to Farnborough Hospital but I hoped that Farnborough would agree to send me home after the observation period. The thought of a long stay at Farnborough was scary because the place didn't offer the conditions for a pleasant, relaxed stay. In hindsight, the doctor who had imagined me dilating had done me a favour because a long a stay in the noisy, overheated wards of Farnborough would have been exhausting.

Doctors at both hospitals discussed my case and agreed I could leave. The paperwork was done for the transfer between hospitals, and I was ready to be discharged. I almost wished I lived nearby and could come back to Queen Charlotte for the delivery. On the other hand, I wanted to be under the care of Mr. Smith.

I travelled in an ambulance for the second time but by day and I was more alert. I was further on in my pregnancy and more confident about reaching thirty-two weeks. And that's what I kept telling myself: visualise and make it real. By thirty-two weeks the baby's organs have formed completely. Twenty-four weeks is the first point of viability. Thirty weeks the first point of normalcy.

In Farnborough Hospital, I was met by a doctor from Mr. Smith's team. Friendly, comforting, as if reading my mind, the first thing she said was she would start me on erythromycin again. The second was that I could go home that very afternoon. I was jubilant. This was the best outcome possible. I had prepared myself for at least forty-eight hours.

Finally, I was coming home. My father had made a little placard saying *Welcome Home* and that night I was delighted to be back in my own bed. Of all the things I had missed, my comfortable, large bed was the biggest. The hospital beds were narrow and firm.

I still had to be closely monitored. I needed one scan and two blood tests a week and a weekly appointment with Mr. Smith.

He was back to his cheerful self now the worst case scenario was over. He had been right about the placenta movement on the day I had the massive bleed. It had moved as he had predicted and was lying correctly now. Unfortunately, though, my baby was lying in breech position. Because of the low fluid, the possibility of SCID and hence risks of infection, Mr. Smith felt the safest thing to do was set a date for a Caesarean. It would be the day I was thirty-six weeks, officially full term.

'Will I be able to carry on that long?' I asked him.

'Yes, why not. You will be fine. I will come and operate,' he promised.

12

I was a little over thirty weeks and I couldn't fit into the few clothes I'd bought. I could have been carrying twins, my stomach looked so big. My best outfit was a pair of checked pink pyjamas that my parents had brought from India. Looking or feeling attractive was far from my mind, unlike last time when I'd worried about the size of my waist, the stretch marks, how I'd lose weight afterwards. This time none of that mattered. My mind ran on fluid loss, how I could control it, how I could ensure the baby continued to thrive. These were my only thoughts.

'Maybe buying a few bits and pieces wouldn't hurt,' my parents said. I was still reluctant, still superstitious about buying much, but my increasing girth and a desire to visit the shops I loved, persuaded me. My husband drove us to Next where I made a few prudent purchases – a couple of pairs of maternity trousers, a couple of tops. I needed clothes for my hospital appointments after all. Then Mothercare. Smart dresses, denim, sexy tops and baby boy t-shirts hung on the rails. I avoided them. I didn't know. I still wasn't sure.

Even though the car was parked close to the shops, I worried. 'I feel I'm leaking,' I said. 'I don't want to be out anymore. Let's go home.'

They looked disappointed. They had hoped that the shops would cheer me up and take my mind off the constant fluid and water routine. They thought I was worrying unreasonably but I felt a growing panic as I registered a lot of leaking fluid, something I hadn't felt for ages.

We went home.

There, I knew I was right. The liquid in the toilet bowl seemed to have other bits in it, like particles. Epithelial cells, I told myself. Epithelial cells, the large squat cells on the skin. Was my baby shedding them? I didn't know if it was possible and still don't know but at that moment, I felt bits of my baby were coming away.

My other problem was constipation. Given my sedentary life, it was fairly predictable. And to prevent the risk of DVT, I wore medical stockings all day. The hospital was insistent but I didn't bother once I got home.

That evening, I felt distinctly uncomfortable.

'My back is hurting from this constipation,' I mumbled. And I was convinced the leaking had increased.

Later that night, I had a very mild bleed, sharp, shiny red.

We rushed to the hospital. They hooked me up to the machine that checked contractions. My baby's heart was beating strongly but they couldn't detect contractions. The doctor on duty, one of Mr. Smith's team, looked uncertain.

'I think we should keep you in for observation. Just in case. But there are no beds free tonight. You will have to stay here, in the labour room.'

It was a huge room, definitely preferable to the noisy, hot wards. I didn't want to stay for weeks though.

'Let us give you the second dose of the steroid today. It's a good time as you are over 31 weeks. And you must promise me, if you feel even the slightest bit uncomfortable, you must come back, even if it's in ten minutes time. Please don't feel embarrassed. Please don't think you are being silly. Remember, just come back.'

'We live very close. Only ten minutes away. We will come back if I feel uncomfortable,' we promised.

We had a private appointment with Mr. Smith in his clinic the following evening. Even though I'd seen him in out-patients, we wanted this extra appointment for the reassurance of another scan. That was another reason I was allowed home.

I was so relieved to be home, but all the next day I was terribly uncomfortable. I couldn't lie down. I blamed the constipation for the umpteenth time.

That evening, we were back with Mr. Smith. The scan was fine. He said that the fluid level wasn't normal but it was enough. He could see my baby swishing around happily.

When I got off the table, I felt a wetness and saw a damp patch on the paper sheet. I was leaking a lot but Mr. Smith still wasn't concerned. I asked what would happen if I suddenly went into labour and he assured me I could call him on his mobile.

'Any time,' he said.

At home, my discomfort increased.

'It's just the constipation. My back,' I said.

My husband cynically asked if I had been reading something new on the net about back pain. I hadn't. The pain in my back and the discomfort increased.

13

It was past midnight, and having not slept from the pain, I got up to the toilet and saw some drops of bright red blood. Solid, deep. I told my husband and he sprang into action. We woke my harassed parents to say we were off to the hospital again.

'They will keep me there,' I said. I had escaped yesterday but this time there would be no way out. I took an overnight bag.

It was very cold but we were oblivious of everything. I don't remember if the night was clear or there were clouds. In five minutes, we were at the hospital. I struggled to get out of the car.

'I think I need a wheelchair. I can hardly walk. So painful.'

My husband looked incredulous. 'It's so close. Only a few steps more.'

So I struggled to the maternity ward.

Once again, they sprang into action. Once again, I was strapped up. The nurse called the doctor. After ten minutes, I couldn't bear it. I was so uncomfortable, so restless. I had to get up for the toilet. The nurse came to unstrap me.

My husband was looking out of the window. 'Look at that! It's snowing.'

It had felt cold but we hadn't thought to check the forecast, so caught up were we in our own events. The snow fell so thick and fast that we would have struggled to get to the hospital had we set off half an hour later.

I didn't look. I was too busy hobbling to the bathroom.

Who would have thought constipation could be this bad? I felt a great urge to push. I sat on the toilet. Something burst. Something gushed. I stood up in horror. Now what would I see?

It was my water breaking. Much, much more than last time. A huge expulsion of water, slightly greenish, or perhaps that was the light. My waters have broken again, I thought, but is that possible when they've already broken? Had the fluid increased that much, the logical bit of my brain asked. I was so used to facing whatever my body pushed out and staying calm, I walked out and found a nurse.

'I think my water just broke. Again,' I said.

The nurse looked alarmed. She rushed to the toilet. I had the sense to leave it there.

'Yes, it is your waters. You are in labour,' she told me. A fact. Again, she strapped me to the machine. 'The doctor will be here any minute.'

The pain. The pain. It came in waves. It completely took over. I felt a strong urge to push. Were these contractions? Were these contractions all along when I thought they were constipation?

So this was it. This would be the night when our lives would change forever. We could only hope. We could only pray. *Om trayambakam, yaja mahe*...my mind moved in auto pilot mode into the *Maha Mrutyunjaya* mantra.

The doctor came rushing in, the same doctor we'd met the previous night. She took one look at me and said she had to do an internal examination.

'And err...is it safe...with the possibility of infection?' I was asking the same question even though I was on the brink. The moment had arrived.

'We need to rush her for a C-section now,' the doctor said.

'We need to call Mr. Smith,' I said. 'We must.'

My husband looked very embarrassed. 'It's kind of four-in-the-morning. We can't disturb him at this time...'

'But he said we could call him whatever the time. We must.'

The doctor said we most certainly could. Apparently, because I was a private patient, it was within my right to do so.

My husband looked at me as if I was mad. It wasn't the first time, of course, but this time he couldn't object so he went to a corner of the room to make the call. It went to voicemail, as expected. He left a message with a lot of, 'Err, hmm, it's late, but since she is in labour...'

'Is she like a centimetre dilated?' he came back and asked.

The doctor and nurse laughed. 'A centimetre? She is way beyond that. She is about to give birth. Any minute. We need to rush.'

And rush they did. Someone ran alongside me as they raced the bed to the operating theatre, trying at the same time to get my signature on the consent forms.

'The bottles...for baby's blood...' I said.

'We have it. Don't worry. We were always ready for you,' I was told.

In the operating theatre, they asked me to sit up, spine bent, like a ball. My mind, which seemed to have a mine of medical memories, remembered that the pain of a spinal injection was the worst. In the story I'd read, a woman had prepared herself mentally for days to survive this ordeal. All I felt was a mild jab. Given the pain I was in, it was nothing.

The anaesthetist, a tall, smiling man, stood at my head, along with my husband. I couldn't see the doctors behind the screens they had put up but I could hear them sometimes. I drifted in and out. There were some jokes. Some laughter. Talk of the snow. No one was able to get in and out of the hospital. The doctor had been here for thirty-six hours but couldn't leave till the next shift arrived. FM radio played early morning songs. I heard one I loved but now, however hard I try, I can't remember which one it was. For some reason, that still bothers me, that I can't tune in to the exact moment with that song.

I still tried to say my mantra but my concentration wavered.

14

'The baby is out!' A clear voice announced, cutting into my hazy thoughts. It was the anaesthetist.

It hadn't seemed long. Contrary to what I'd imagined, a caesarean was a quick operation of about thirty minutes.

'The baby is out, but why isn't he crying?' I whispered. Or perhaps I shouted. I was so drugged I didn't know. It was the moment of truth. Had we been wrong in taking such a huge gamble? Playing with life and death? What did we know, after all, with our hope and faith and prayers and a few stories of miracles?

If he is cold, born still, how will you heal? How can you ever heal?

And then a loud cry echoed round the room. It burst into my heart. The miracle had happened. My little baby boy was here.

I saw him only for a second. He was wheeled out very quickly, in what looked like a giant incubator, a large contraption hooked up to various machines, including a ventilator. All I thought was: He is fine. His lungs have formed. He is safe.

Later my husband would tell me how those moments of silence – thirty seconds or a minute or longer – had everyone holding their breath. The nurse smacked the baby on his bottom – silence. The doctor whispered, Oh no, oh no, and smacked him, palms loud on his bottom, harder and harder, ten times, fifteen times perhaps, while holding him upside down. And then a loud cry burst into the room. Smiles flashed and the tension dissolved. For me, semi-conscious from the drugs, it felt like no time at all between the shout, 'Baby's out', my question, and that cry of life, but for the others in the operating theatre, those moments were long ones of shock, concern and finally palpable relief. I was wheeled to the recovery ward to wait until my room was ready. On my trolly-bed, near the window, lying back on the pillows, I could see the gentle snow covering the countryside. How incredible, how fitting that he was born on such a beautiful day. I was also gearing up to feel the pain like last time, but I felt nothing. They had put me on some strong painkillers.

My husband went to see our baby and returned, all smiles. My questions poured out. How was he? Was everything all right? Absolutely all right? No bent foot? No squashed nose? Nothing wrong? Nothing?

'He just has a birthmark on his left arm. Apart from that, he's fine. Perfect. In fact, they think they'll be able to take him off the ventilator in the next hour or so. They think he can breathe without support.'

'Already? And will he be on CPAP[15] then?' I gasped.

I knew from the successful deliveries in the PPROM group that the CPAP, in spite of its scary sounding acronym, was a simple machine which helped with breathing if the airways were blocked. If he could be moved from ventilator to CPAP support in only a few hours, it was an extremely positive development.

His blood samples had been sent by special delivery, never

15 CPAP: Continuous Positive Airway Pressure

mind the snow, to Great Ormond Street. We were staying positive that he was SCID free.

By midday, I had been taken to a big single room. In the evening, my husband visited our baby in the neonatal intensive care unit and then came to see me.

'The blood results are back,' he said.

It had to be the top right quadrant of the graph. Positive thoughts, prayers, wishes. It had to be.

Instead, he said hesitantly, 'If I tell you that he too has SCID, will you be very upset?'

For one mad moment, I hoped he was joking, but his face said it all.

A roll of the dice. Unlucky again?

SECTION 5 – REGENERATION – HOPE

1

It is hard to describe what I felt at that time. A sinking sensation and a complete dread that the word SCID was back in our lives. I reminded myself that I knew children who had had a bone marrow transplant and were well. That we were in the right place at the right time. There was hope. Then exhaustion at the thought of yet another journey ahead, after the prolonged endometriosis, the ruptured membranes. I thought, 'If only. If only my body had passed on the good X. If only my mind could have influenced my body.

'Do they know?' I asked, as my parents approached my bedside. They had been to the neonatal with my husband.

'No, I haven't said anything. Why not wait a couple of days before we tell them? The final results will be back by then.'

'Is there any chance there might be a mistake? What will the final results tell us?' I asked. The message from Great Ormond Street said that based on the very quick blood test, there was a high probability that our baby had SCID but was there a possibility that my miracle baby would somehow prove them wrong?

'I don't know…the doctor in the neonatal unit who spoke to GOSH seemed very certain about it.'

I told my parents, right then, rather abruptly, because I didn't know what else to do. They, like everyone else, had felt it couldn't possibly happen again. Bad things happened to people, but not twice. God couldn't and wouldn't do that to us.

They were speechless in disbelief. Again? The unlucky dice, again?

I didn't want to think about what God did and why. I reminded myself of my own theory of the soul's chosen path of struggle. Over the years, I had read many books from different cultures which tried to make sense of personal grief in an impersonal universe. I'd stitched theories and phrases and developed my own – that everyone's journey is unique and that the joys ahead for me are different from those of others. If my soul has chosen a journey towards motherhood that includes hardship and struggles, I will be supported along the way. If I accept these challenges, I will find a way of making my dreams a reality. I also reminded myself about positive visualisation and how I believed in it, how it had worked for me before. I tried to assure myself that the baby who had survived, even though statistics had said he wasn't meant to, would come through the transplant process perfectly fine. The struggle wasn't over yet. The fight would continue. But victory was certain. I tried to focus my thoughts but they remained jumbled and scared.

The nurse arrived with a syringe and asked me if I needed any more painkillers. The memory of the burning pain from my first C-section, eight years ago, was still raw. I couldn't face that again.

'Please,' I said, holding out my arm for the injection.

'Any time you are in pain, please let us know. We'll give you pain relief,' she said kindly.

A catheter hung out of me, a steady dripping. I didn't even look down. The doctor who had performed the operation came to check me. She said it had been her most complicated caesarean with several adhesions due to the endometriosis. That was why the catheter was still in. Usually it was used only during the operation and for short time afterwards.

'How long does this have to stay in? It wasn't really painful but I could feel it there, a little tube connected somewhere inside.

'Until the liquid runs clear. Then we will be sure there is no internal bleeding.'

There was enough to think and worry about so I didn't add this latest problem to my list. Before I knew it, I fell into a dreamless sleep. I wasn't aware of my parents and husband leaving.

The news next morning was that my baby had been well all night in his incubator. He was well established on CPAP probes to aid breathing which would be removed later in the evening. That was incredible news and meant that his lungs were fine. Certainly fine.

2

A midwife came to see me later that morning. She was tall and big but with a gentle manner and was dismayed that I hadn't seen my baby yet.

'Didn't anyone bring him to you?'

'They can't! He's premature. He needs to be in an incubator.'

'Of course, silly of me to ask. But why hasn't anyone taken you to see him?'

'I can't get up. There's no way I can walk all that way. I hear it's quite far.'

'It's a bit silly, isn't it, to have the neonatal unit so far from the maternity ward? Let's see what we can do.'

'I can't take a step,' I protested. I imagined being forced to walk. The pain of eight years ago returned as raw as if were yesterday. If I tried to get up now, I would feel that horrible burning, like a tearing inside me. My body felt like it was cut in half.

'You may not be able to walk, but we have wheelchairs, don't we? We must take you to see your baby.' She said she would speak to Claire, the chief midwife who had visited me in the early days of my pregnancy and whom I'd called the day after my waters broke. She knew my case.

They came back triumphant. They had found a wheelchair. Then the next step. 'Don't you want to shower and freshen up a bit to see your baby?'

'Err, can I? I mean this stuff is attached to me,' I looked down at the catheter still dripping red.

'We can't yet remove it but I'll hold the bag and we can get you to the shower.'

But the thought of that filled me with panic.

'Err, hmm, won't it take a long time? Don't you have somewhere to go?'

'I am staying here with you until we get you to see your baby and back,' she said firmly and came over to my side.

I had to try, for her sake. She was doing this for me. I tried gingerly to lift myself up. I moved and waited to feel the slicing pain, but she was still smiling patiently.

'Let's try to sit up now.'

I thought I had been sitting up halfway but I had made little progress. I was so numb I could hardly figure what I was doing.

'Deep breaths,' she went on, trying to encourage me. Of course she didn't know the years of fear that were trapped inside me and which held me back. I imagined most women would be sitting up unflinching by now.

Somehow I managed, I got out of bed, holding on to her hand. But in the shower, she told me to stand a little straighter and started to leave to give me some privacy. She would be right outside the shower curtains, holding on to the catheter.

I couldn't do it. 'It's too painful. I can't.' I was bent double.

'OK, never mind, we can try later. Let's take you to see your baby now.' Her manner, so calm, so kind, made me think she wouldn't label me as a wimp no matter what I did.

I hobbled and sank into the wheelchair. Anyone who's had a caesarean will know that when you sit or stand, you feel the cut. You know your body has been stitched in an awkward place. I'd

234

had my morning painkillers. Three tablets. The more the better, I thought.

'What about the injection?' I asked. 'Can I have that as well?'

'No, my dear. You've already had two doses so we can't give you any more.'

But I needed the injection! Not only would it take away the pain, it would make me feel more relaxed.

Noticing my disappointment perhaps, she explained. 'It's morphine. We are not allowed to give you more than two doses. These tablets should do you fine now but let us know if you don't feel better.'

I must have had a very complex operation to be given morphine. No wonder it had knocked me out so well and made me feel human.

I managed to get into the wheelchair with her help, holding on to the catheter, with its large plastic bag of red liquid, as there was nowhere else to put it. She pushed me into the long corridor. I was in my hospital gown, white with a faint blue print, tied at the back. It was a cold but bright day. My baby's little face was indistinct in my mind. Now I would finally see him.

I knew the rules of entry into the neonatal unit from my time in Queen Charlotte – the thorough washing of hands and removal of all jewellery and outer footwear before you could go through. The lives behind the doors were precious and fragile.

The neonatal unit, or PICU as it was called here, had three rooms; one ward, one double room and a single room for the most vulnerable. This is where my baby was. She wheeled me into the large room. The incubator with all its machines and screens was on the right. The curtain was drawn and it was quite dark, as it needed to be because premature babies don't like bright light. The midwife opened the curtain just a little. She pushed me close to the incubator and whispered, 'I will come back in a while to take you back.' She seemed delighted to be doing this for me, giving me that moment when a mother sees her baby for the first time.

Now, alone, I looked at him. He lay on his back, his face a little to one side. We hadn't bought any baby clothes, first because he was early and second because we didn't know if he would ever need them. If he would even live. The hospital had dressed him in a light blue babygrow, very big for him and with openings on one side. The feet of the body suit were unfilled because his own little feet were much smaller. A feeding tube was inserted in his nose, but I expected that. A cannula on his foot. I expected that as well. I too had a cannula in my right arm and knew that they are routine. He was sleeping peacefully, oblivious of the paraphernalia around him, and on his face – the look! A look of such confidence, as if to say, 'I am here now. I am fine and in your care. I will be safe.' I stared at him in wonder. So this little one was my miracle baby. Four pounds at birth. A good weight considering how early he was but still small compared with the eight pound babies other women boasted of. So small and with so much confidence. So much trust in me and in the world. He seemed happy, and also proud as if he was telling me, *Mummy, here I am! You promised you would hold, and you did and so did I.* A perfect baby, but with one massive imperfection which meant he would need a bone marrow transplant. They would give him chemotherapy, his beautiful hair would fall out, the cannula would remain for ages, a feeding button placed in his stomach for years. A donor would have to be found. We would have to go to Great Ormond Street Hospital after all. As these thoughts filled my head, I felt the world spin. I was dehydrated and I felt dizzy. Perhaps I had shouted out, 'Excuse me,' or maybe they noticed me slump.

A nurse was there asking me, 'Are you all right?'

'Yes, yes, I am fine, just felt faint. The exhaustion I think.'

'It is a lot to take in,' she said. All the nurses were so kind and understanding.

The midwife came back for me. 'He's so gorgeous,' she said.

'Thank you! I almost fainted just then.'

'Aww, bless you. You have gone through so much. Now let's get you back. Maybe you can come back to see him in the evening.'

She thought the promise of a visit would motivate me to start walking while I was hoping I could keep the wheelchair until I left the hospital.

'Did you get a chance to give him a cuddle?' she asked.

'Oh no, I didn't think he could be taken out of the incubator.'

'That's a shame.' She looked disappointed. I wondered what she would have made of Woodland nursing home practice of leaving new born babies in a nursery. I wanted to tell her the story, but I was so tired.

3

That evening, my husband's work colleagues visited with a massive bunch of flowers. Large lilies and some purple flowers whose name I didn't know were held together with a white satin ribbon. They had been very supportive of my husband and all the time he had taken off for appointments and hospital visits. I thanked them for their help, their wishes, and the bitter Korean brew that was my companion through all the days. They didn't know that there would be more visits to come in another hospital.

The flowers were placed on the windowsill. Later, a nurse would come with a picture of my baby, sleeping comfortably despite all the breathing and feeding tubes. 'There, now you can see your gorgeous baby whenever you want,' she said, resting it against the flowers.

The nurses asked me if I wanted to breastfeed. A premature baby wouldn't have the strength to feed so I would have to regularly express milk and the only way to maintain a supply of milk was to use a breast pump. Did I want to breastfeed? I remembered well how it felt, the utter contentment of a little body reliant on me, the comfort my little baby got as he lay cradled in my arms. There was sheer bliss in knowing that I was providing for another human being and the happiness of shutting myself off from the world of sales targets and work and bosses. As a career oriented feminist, I never imagined I would enjoy it.

Yet, after all these years of yearning for what was lost, this was the one feeling I missed and wished desperately to have again. Of those moments, of just me and my baby, of being in our own beautiful world with his little contented sounds. Did I want it all again? It was not even a question. And there was a medical advantage. One of the main reasons SCID babies became ill at four or five months was because they were being weaned so the immunity passed on in the mother's milk was lost. I said yes. I was determined to help my baby as much as I could.

They brought me a breast pump and bottles. The plan was that they would freeze the milk until my baby was strong enough to drink from a bottle.

They finally removed the catheter two days after the delivery. The nurse warned me that though it would take only a second to yank out, it would hurt. Given that the medical community thought nothing hurt, when they said it would hurt, I was bracing myself.

'OK, deep breaths. One, two, three,' she said and pulled it out.

She was right. It was a blinding pain but over very quickly.

Mr. Smith visited me, delighted his treatment had worked but concerned that our journey with doctors and hospitals wasn't over. He was like the friend who always gave you his complete attention, the one you could whinge to. When he said goodbye, it felt like the end of an era after two years attending his clinics, even though I had an appointment for my post-operative follow-up as well as regular scans to check for endometriosis over the coming years.

4

In the evening, a couple of my friends came to visit with gifts for the baby. They couldn't see him because visitors were not allowed in the neonatal unit so they had to be content with the unusual set up of being with the mother without her baby, and a mother who did not want to speak to anyone.

When I lay on the bed that evening, I could see my stomach moving, the crushed pulpy skin heaving as if there was another baby inside. For one moment, I wondered if there could be, but given the number of scans I'd had, the doctors would have been completely blind to have missed it. So many people couldn't have made a mistake.

With no more morphine injections, I had to be content with frequent doses of codeine and ibuprofen. I wanted to numb myself and not feel any pain. Weeks later, a friend would explain it to me. 'You had a tough time losing your baby last time and let's face it, this pregnancy was no cakewalk at all. In your mind and body, pregnancy and birth is therefore associated with extreme pain.' Perhaps that explained why so many women walked out of hospital within two days of a caesarean – something I couldn't even contemplate.

In the middle of the night I woke up needing the toilet. As soon as I sat down, something poured out of me. One scared glance revealed a slab, a huge chunk of solid blood. It slipped out, a pound of flesh, a part of my insides pushed out. I managed to get back to the bed and called a nurse. When she came – I was a high alert patient so they came quickly – and went to the toilet, I heard a gasp. She emerged holding the mound in gloved hands.

'How are you otherwise?'

'I feel a bit better, thank you. What is it, do you think?'

'I don't know. Maybe they left something inside.' She was clearly worried but remained calm. 'I will tell the doctors. You may need to go back to surgery to check everything is fine inside.'

If I have to, I will, I thought. What else could I do?

'I will be back soon to clear it up,' she said.

I tried to sleep. The lilies had a heady smell so my room was nicely scented. It wasn't as hot and uncomfortable as in the wards. I'd heard stories of women still in pain from giving birth and from C-sections being left with the baby, unable to sit up to feed them or change nappies. They had to listen to the babies crying all night when they were exhausted and wrung out. My baby and I were looked after. Looking in from outside, perhaps some would say I was very lucky.

There was no sign of the nurse and I had to go to the toilet again. With a fair amount of trepidation I went, but there was only a little more blood. I pressed the buzzer again and waited.

She came after a long time, when I had almost fallen asleep. She looked mortified. 'I am so sorry, I was supposed to come and clean up, but it is so busy tonight. You shouldn't have had to use the toilet when it was in such a state. I am really sorry.'

The blood was everywhere. It was not pleasant.

'It's all right.'

'No, it's my fault. I should have come back but there's not a minute's rest tonight.' Perhaps she expected me to complain and shout. Outside I could hear another buzzer go off. I looked at her harried face. This is what people complained about with the NHS. But what did she know of the journey I had been through? What did her being late matter when your baby was in the neonatal care unit, about to be sent to Great Ormond Street? Perspective shapes one's reaction. In the end, life hones you into who you are. Later, when friends complained about their stays in maternity wards, I would smile quietly to myself. One woman complained about a nurse who suggested she tie back her long, loose hair before she went into labour. Another said the nurses didn't respond quickly enough to her buzzer. But for every person not urgently needing help, there was probably someone like me who was at high risk and did need attention. How could you blame such hard working people?

5

My husband brought news after more discussions. Great Ormond Street was waiting to admit us but, although a children's hospital, it didn't have a dedicated neonatal unit because premature babies were cared for in the local hospitals. While my baby was still on breathing support and needed to be on CPAP, they couldn't admit him. On the other hand, they worried that the longer he was in the local hospital, the higher risk of infection. They were stressing the need for isolation.

The third day brought news of jaundice, fairly common with young babies, even normal ones. A day under a strong white light was enough, and he recovered soon. I visited him every day without a wheel chair. I found that if I walked slowly I didn't experience searing pain. It was only a little when I got in and out of bed or had to bend. I was doing much better than last time because I was tanked up with painkillers.

My baby's room overlooked the car park. It was usually quiet in the neonatal centre, the silence broken only when a loud alarm sounded and everyone rushed to answer it. Usually the reason was that a baby's air saturation level had fallen below the safe mark. Every baby in the neonatal unit was monitored day and night. A small clip attached to a toe read saturation levels and checked heart functions. Regular blood tests monitored haemoglobin levels. There was a rigorous policy of hand washing and wearing aprons. It was almost like an isolation unit. I wondered why Great Ormond was worrying about inadequate isolation and risk of infection in the local hospital.

The nurse asked, 'Would you like to change his nappy?'

'Um, can I? There are so many tubes and things, I mean, should I?' He looked so small and fragile.

'Of course you can. You will be perfectly fine.' She left me alone with him, saying she would be back after checking on something else.

I knew they encouraged bonding. Premature babies craved the warmth of the human body. They needed to be held and cradled. I thought of my first baby in a nursery, nowhere near me. My new baby had less reason to be near me. He was a bubble boy, the name given to X-SCID babies because of the isolation and the lack of human contact. Here, everyone was making sure we spent as much time as we could together.

I carefully moved his little foot with the cannula. 'Ouch, I hope that didn't hurt?' He slept on blissfully.

The first time I needed a cannula, I'd held my arm stiff all day, thinking a needle was inside, not a thin tube through which a needle could be inserted whenever needed. I knew better now. I understood that these attachments were necessary to help my baby. A massive cannula on his tiny foot, a feeding tube through his little nose, the CPAP over his nostrils. I bent over him, almost into the incubator, and gently started to remove the nappy. The lift of the little legs, the sliding out of the nappy from underneath the bum, the wiping with the tissue. It could have been yesterday, not seven years ago. It all came back. Then suddenly I was panicking because the wipes were nowhere to be seen, nor the new nappies. Of course, they had to be on the table next to the incubator but how was I supposed to bend and pick them up? Should I put his legs down? Just as I was wondering what to do next, he had the biggest poo ever. A baby with nasal feeding will poo in much larger quantities than normal. It made my predicament worse, bending over him, trying to get to the wipes and a clean nappy. In future, I would keep things next to me. First lesson learnt. It took me double the time but finally I managed. The nurse came back just when I'd managed to get a clean baby into a new nappy.

'Sorry I was a bit held up. Did you get on OK?'

'He did a big poo…and it took me so long to change him.' I was like a child telling her parents about the tough time she'd had on her first day at school. I was sweating from the effort in the warm room.

'But you did so well, didn't you? I knew you would!'

It was this gentle, polite encouragement about the smallest things that kept me going. Instead of pointing out the obvious – *it's your baby, you need to do this* – most of the nurses and doctors encouraged me at every little step.

I was not ready or prepared to be discharged. I was happy in my single room with the smell of the lilies. At home, I would have to climb stairs, sleep on a non-adjustable bed. Hospitals with their sense of community and routine could be appealing!

My baby was off the breathing probes and had remained stable for a whole day. This meant he could breathe on his own, unaided. They sent word to Great Ormond and their reply was quick.

They would send an ambulance the next day to take him to London.

6

The ambulance arrived late in the afternoon. My parents and I were in the neonatal unit, waiting to see my baby off. He was dressed in the new babygrow we had bought. My husband had done some hasty shopping in the local Mothercare. Only clothes in the *early baby* range fitted, tiny clothes that would later fit one of his soft toys. One was striped with the words *Little but loud*. The nurses didn't know how much their light-hearted comment meant to us – 'Goodness, I am going deaf. He certainly has a loud cry, doesn't he?'

He was ready, dressed in his going out clothes, a thicker dark blue body suit, eyes shut, still with a look of supreme confidence on his face, such a little face, such a resolutely strong face. The ambulance crew was a young man and woman. Could I trust them to take this precious child across London? Would the driver drive carefully? I imagined all kinds of dreadful scenarios.

'Is it all right for him to travel alone?'

'He is not alone. We are fully trained paramedics,' the girl said, matter of fact.

My mother was in tears. 'How can he go alone? You go with him,' she told me, a bit irrationally.

The girl heard her. 'The mother can't travel because she is a patient. She needs to be discharged from the hospital first. We can't manage two patients in the ambulance.'

Next, my mother asked my father, 'Why don't you go with them?'

'We've been instructed to take no-one else in the ambulance. Only the parents if they are able. Not grandparents,' the girl said firmly.

My husband was working in London so he could be at Great Ormond Street to meet our baby. But this journey across London was his own.

The girl's manner was brusque, but her touch was gentle as she placed my baby very carefully into the transporting unit.

We walked out to the ambulance parked outside. My baby remained peacefully asleep and I was reassured by the huge contraption he was in, a machine to look after every possible eventuality.

'OK, Mum, we are ready to go, so if you want to say bye…,' the girl told me.

I reached out my hand to touch the unit. There was nothing else I could do.

'I will go to see him as soon as I'm discharged from here,' I said. Not that it made any difference to her and the other ambulance staff.

They drove off. The three of us returned to my room, very subdued.

Later in the evening, my husband called. The ambulance had arrived safely and our baby was in his room, Number 6 in Robin Ward. My husband sounded jubilant. He spoke about how kind the nurses were, how fantastic the hospital was, how everyone was wonderful, how they had all been waiting for our child. How they all said he was cute.

'The nurses here are kind as well,' I said, puzzled that he sounded so happy.

'Oh, they are, but the people here! They are just all so wonderful. You will love it.'

'It's not a holiday resort, is it?' I was cross. And upset.

'I met Dr. Williams as well. She remembered you.'

'She's still there?'

All those years before, Dr. Williams had responded to my desperate plea from across the world. My world had changed so much that it was hard to believe the same people were still there.

With my baby in a different hospital, I felt lonely. A bit without purpose, here without a reason. They still hadn't said anything about discharging me but I was surely reaching the end of my welcome. I had been there for five days.

The next morning the doctors told me I could leave the following day. I was desperate to get home and on to Great Ormond Street.

Like the third and final continent.[16]

---

16 The third and final continent: Interpreter of Maladies by Jhumpa Lahiri

8

When we moved to London in March 2001, we had bought a London pass for two days during the Easter weekend and visited the sights just like tourists. We wanted to do it before we settled in and started taking the city for granted. One place I had wanted to see was Great Ormond Street Hospital. I remember it was raining hard and we walked up from Russell Square tube station after visiting the British Museum. A few twists and turns and there it was. A greyish building at the end of the road. I had stood staring at it, my symbol of hope that had never come to fruition.

Eight years later we were once again standing outside Great Ormond Street Hospital, but in very different circumstances and with a different baby boy. Had we made it here last time, it would have been as a helpless couple with a desperately ill child, in debt to kind strangers who'd donated money. Now we lived in one of the best cities in the world and called it home. We didn't have to worry about raising funds, and our baby was infection free which made his chances of recovery significantly higher. I acknowledged our blessings.

My memory seemed hazy because looking at the building now, on a cold sunny day, it appeared different. It wasn't at the end of a road so much as spread out all along Great Ormond Street. A blue-topped glass dome covered the walkway to the main building, possibly a new addition. The road was busy with cars and ambulances.

My husband led the way, talking non-stop about the different areas of the hospital. Up the lifts to the fourth floor and we were at the doors of Robin Ward. The first thing I noticed was the antibacterial gel dispensers placed on the walls. *Please wash your hands* with pictures showing the proper way to do it. I guiltily remembered laughing at some acquaintances in India who were paranoid about washing their hands well. Hand washing was here to stay in our lives, as it should.

Then another set of doors and we were at the reception. The nurses wore blue uniforms. They smiled widely as if they already knew me.

And then the room. Double glass doors. A sink and gel after the first door where you washed your hands again.

'But I haven't touched anything since I've entered.'

'It doesn't matter, you have to. You can't do it enough,' my husband said, washing his hands again and handing me the plastic apron we had to wear when we were in the room. A push of the inner door and we were inside. The air itself was triple filtered which was why Great Ormond wanted our child here as soon as possible. They tried to replicate the *bubble* as best as they could. Already I could see big differences in this set up and the room in Farnborough.

Our baby slept in the middle of the large room, in a large cot, not in a closed incubator. He was lying on top of an open heated plate which kept him warm. A humongous machine stood next to his bed, a sentinel checking his breathing levels, heart beat and so on. He had a cannula on his little hand – so they'd removed the one on the foot, and put in a new one – but who had comforted him when he cried? Brave, brave baby, all on his own, with so much confidence in the adults around him. He was only five days old and premature by eight weeks. He stayed asleep most of the day, perhaps thinking he was still in his mother's womb.

Once again, I thought of he who had come before and who had lain in an open room in Vellore with no air-conditioning and no isolation. What chance did he have? Even if we had managed to get him to London, he might never have made a complete recovery. My first born. He would have been eight years old. It hurt to think of him. It hurt not to.

Later in the morning, Dr. Williams arrived with other doctors on her team. I launched into my back story of how years ago I had written to her and how we had been desperate to come to London. She remembered and said they were happy we were here now and were safe. Another doctor spoke briefly about the treatment.

'First, we have to find a donor and we'd like to wait until the baby is a few months old. You can probably take him home while we wait. Once we find the donor, we will do a cycle of chemotherapy to effectively kill all his existing cells and then we can carry out the bone marrow transplant. There's a risk that he might develop a reaction to the transplant called the graft-vs-host disease when the host cells attack the graft. We will have to monitor him closely for almost a month after the transplant but the T-cells should soon start coming back. The B-cells will take a little longer, perhaps a couple of months.'

I had heard of graft-vs-host disease. Several of the children in my SCID support group had contracted it. It was one of the worst worries after a transplant.

'His hair will all go,' the doctor said cheerfully, 'and he has so much of it!'

'Will it grow back?' I asked.

'Of course it will! There will be some other side effects however.'

'One of the problems of chemotherapy is that it affects fertility. So there's a possibility that he won't be able to father a child,' Dr. Williams added.

We nodded.

In front of us was a little baby for whom we wanted a healthy life. His own babies were too far away in the future. So what if he couldn't? Many couples couldn't have babies. They could always adopt. Maybe the girl he was with wouldn't want babies, who knew? That could have been a problem anyway, SCID notwithstanding. Infertility wasn't a major hurdle. My thoughts were drifting. The pain in my stomach was coming back.

'Do you mind if I sit down?' I asked. There was only one chair in the room and it was at the other corner. They were apologetic. Of course, I had had an operation. I needed to sit down.

They continued listing the possible problems. The donor database didn't contain enough people from the Asian gene pool. The chances of finding a good match for an Indian child were therefore lower than for others. A sibling was the best hope but of course there was none.

'What about cousins?'

'Unfortunately not the same as siblings.'

We suggested asking friends and relatives but that wasn't how it worked. The donors had to be registered with the Anthony Nolan Trust.

Later, one of our friends offered to register as a donor. It is only when life threatening things happen that gratitude takes on a whole new meaning. Every word, every gesture, every hospital visit. Our friends will be forever painted in the colours of kindness.

The doctors left on their rounds having told us everything there was to know.

I was tired by the time we got home. The long drive, the mass of new information and my concerns about what lay ahead had exhausted me. My parents were waiting for us but my concerns made me nervous and irritated. The next day I stayed at home. It would be the weekend before my husband would drive us to the hospital again. I was in no state to travel on my own.

9

Three weeks after I'd given birth, I returned to Farnborough Hospital for a checkup. On the way back, I called for a cab to take me to the station, and from there I would take a train to London. The driver looked at my stomach, not yet flat, and asked, 'So how many months?'

'I have already had my baby,' I laughed.

He looked back at me. Then I realised his confusion. Here I was with a large tummy telling him I'd had my baby yet there was no baby with me.

'My mother is at home with him,' I lied. I didn't want to start on the long explanation.

He looked even more incredulous. 'Yes, women these days, they get back to their own lives quickly.' His tone suggested he didn't agree with this swanning off to London and leaving my baby behind.

'Just a couple of hours,' I said, sounding defensive, knowing I had no reason to be. I knew that if I told him the truth he would offer sympathy, but I didn't want to share my problems. Sometimes I explained everything to a person serving coffee, sometimes I couldn't confide in a friend sitting opposite me. It happened. I accepted it.

Every day I called Robin Ward as soon as I woke and a cheerful voice would tell me how my baby was, sometimes adding that he was 'desatted'. I ignored this information because only later did I understand that a drop in oxygen saturation level was potentially serious and worrying. The level was constantly monitored via a sensor on his foot which beeped and alerted the team if it dropped below ninety five percent.

I always arrived in the middle of the morning when all the staff were swept up in a whirlwind of care. I would talk to the nurses about his nappy changes, his feeds and further tests. The main focus, they said, was to keep him healthy and infection free until the transplant. He was therefore examined every day for skin and ear infections, thrush in the mouth, a fever and other concerns. The only infection he did get was on his foot after the many heel pricks to take his blood at Farnborough Hospital. IV antibiotics cleared it before it became serious.

One weekend afternoon, we arrived to see that our baby was having a blood transfusion. Even though I knew he had SCID, to see the consequences for myself was shocking and difficult. SCID children often needed blood transfusions. So far, the breathing support, the incubator and the cannulas had been because of prematurity and many babies were born early and had similar problems. But to see a small baby hooked up to a bag of blood for a transfusion was scary. Our first baby had also needed a transfusion in Vellore, and it was then that we understood that if ever he needed a blood transfusion, it would have to be irradiated blood with killed blood cells. For a SCID child, a normal blood transfusion could be fatal.

Otherwise, he was doing well, still the smallest patient in Robin Ward and the most pampered by the entire staff.

10

Every month the rota of doctors changed in the wards, as in every other hospital. It was March and the new doctor on duty came to say hello and called me out for a quick chat. He looked very young. Introducing himself as Dr. Thomas, he told me that they had another idea for the proposed treatment.

'Instead of the traditional bone marrow transplant, we plan to follow a different process. It is called a haplo-identical transplant with stem cells. So instead of looking for a matching donor, we take stem cells from one of the parents.'

'Oh, it's Dr. Radley's method, from Duke University!' I interrupted.

He seemed surprised. 'Yes, she usually uses the same procedure. It's much safer for young babies because there's no chemotherapy.'

'But the B-cells never come back. Children need to have immunoglobulins – IVIG – infusions all their lives.'

He was smiling now, perhaps at my information or earnestness. 'That is indeed true. What we have found is that after chemotherapy there is a complete reconstitution of the immune system but…'

'Yes, both T and B-cells come back. And this is the treatment GOSH uses too,' I interrupted again, determined to show how much I already knew.

'That's right. So, to put it simply, the immune system usually, but not always, reconstitutes itself when the host cells are destroyed and there is space for new cells. However, using stem cells from a parent is a much gentler method because the stem cells are younger cells and do not attack the host.'

'So there is no graft-vs-host disease?'

'That's right.' He was smiling again, in fact he almost chuckled. 'There is usually no severe form of graft-vs-host disease.'

I knew that, of course. I knew Dr. Radley had a much gentler approach. She treated newborn babies, even at a day old. Hadn't my parents suggested we go to America and be treated by her for this very reason?

'But Great Ormond always does chemotherapy. Why would you choose not to in this case?' I'd read enough emails, stories and opinions in my SCID group to ask a question like this.

'We follow different protocols depending on the case. We have done a stem cell transplant on another little boy, and today he is six years old, perfectly healthy. He has complete reconstitution of the T-cells.'

'But the B-cells didn't come back?'

'Not really, but he is a perfectly healthy boy. Last year the family went on a holiday across Asia. They carried all his needles. They do SCIG now subcutaneously.' He didn't bother to explain more because I was nodding my head to show I knew the difference between IVIG and SCIG.

'But at least with the chemo, there would be a complete cure.'

'It depends. Anyway, we are still discussing the different options but I wanted to let you know that this is one possibility.'

I went back to my haven, our filtered room where our baby slept peacefully, thinking I would insist on seeing Dr. Williams before agreeing to anything the new doctor recommended. The decision was critical and I wanted another opinion.

11

The breastfeeding nurse, Mary, a tiny bird-like woman in her sixties was as fierce as she was kind. She came once she knew I was keen to breastfeed and having heard my story, she pledged me her total support. She said she could replace the formula given through the feeding tube with breast milk. My expressed milk would be stored in the freezer, put into bottles, and fed to my baby through the tube.

'There's not much,' I said apologetically. 'Farnborough Hospital only stored a little because I wasn't able to express much in those early days.'

She reassured me that the quantity didn't matter because the first breast milk was rich in vitamins and minerals which helped immunity. She wasn't happy that they hadn't sent it with me and said she would chase it. I explained that my baby had been taken by ambulance and I had been discharged later, but she wasn't accepting any excuses. She marched off to make the necessary calls to ensure my milk reached GOSH.

GOSH ran a scheme whereby a breastfeeding mother was given a voucher worth five pounds each day of her stay to contribute towards meals in the hospital canteen and cafes. Eating out was expensive and they wanted to ensure a lactating mother ate well and healthily. All I had to do was go to the administration office each week and collect vouchers. I did this diligently. The canteen was so heavily subsidised that I could pay for both lunch and dinner with my five-pound voucher.

Mary brought me a much nicer and simpler breast pump and I went back to expressing every day. I had become irregular, often not doing it at home, but now, relaxed in our air filtered cocoon, and with the better breast pump, I did much better. The nurse on duty would take the bottles, date and time stamp them, and put them in a big freezer. The milk was to be stored until the doctors confirmed I didn't have a condition called CMV, a common virus most people had in their blood streams but which was unsafe for a SCID baby. If I had it, then it would be inadvisable to breast feed.

There were frequent blood tests. Sometimes I would find the team of doctors and nurses gathered around my baby's bed, discussing a new test.

'Why don't you step outside and relax?' a nurse would say when they were about to take blood.

'I would rather be here.'

'Are you sure you will be all right?'

I wasn't, but I punished myself. If my baby was going through it, I would be there with him in his pain. It was the least I could do. Once they couldn't find a strong vein in his little foot or his hand. They kept trying different veins and he cried incessantly. My own tears welled up.

'Do you have to do this now? Why does he need this test?' I interjected.

'Would Mum like to step out? Maybe get a cup of tea?' the young doctor responded.

I did, that time. I went to the kitchen to get a cup of tea but

I could hear his cries all the way down the corridor, despite the double doors.

Over the years, I lost one of my email accounts and was no longer part of the SCID group. Eight years later, once again, I typed the word 'JOIN' in the subject line of my email. I wrote a bit about myself and my background. Once again, the responses were quick. Welcoming me back to the family. Congratulating me at the new arrival. Shocked at the journey I had gone through. Supportive that I was in the right place. Relieved that this time there was hope of a transplant. There were many who still remembered me.

It felt like coming home.

I wrote to the NIH to tell them I had another baby with SCID because they had done my free SCID carrier tests. I wrote to Dr. Radley in America, reminding her of my case history, and because the doctors here were still discussing different ways to treat my son.

A friend, whose daughter had been treated in GOSH, came to visit. After my first son's death, the two of us had often discussed discussions about the advantages and disadvantages of different treatments. I complained that Dr. Thomas didn't want to follow the traditional and successful method practiced in Great Ormond Street. Her response surprised me.

'No, not at all. No. Dr. Thomas might look young, but he is highly experienced. He is fantastic. I would trust him with my child's life. Again and again.'

My friend is a courageous, strong soul. She would fight till the end for her daughter so I trusted her recommendation.

I decided I was in good hands.

12

My parents were tired. They had been with us for five months, through all the tension, waiting and cold weather. Visa regulations stated that a visiting foreigner could stay in the country for six months so there wasn't much more time. They had come to look after me and they had done that. I was back on my own two feet and I didn't need to be nursed anymore. My baby was in hospital. They were really homesick. Did they need to stay any longer? I agreed that they should go back home.

'But what about you? Won't you need family around when you go through the transplant? Both of you will need some reassurance, some support, they said. They suggested maybe my in-laws should come. Or maybe one of my husband's siblings, given that he had three.

'Somebody needs to be here when he goes through the difficult times of chemotherapy,' they worried.

I asked the SCID group. Would I need a family member with me given that I would be in hospital for twenty-four hours? My friend, who had gone through the transplant in England while her family was in India, said I would. The days of chemo were long and dark. Then there would be the complications of the graft-vs-host disease. It was a long and trying struggle. It would be nice to have someone there to support you.

I thought about it. Having someone staying with us meant

we would need to look after them as well. My support was here, in this room, with my baby, with my endless prayers, with the doctors who thought only about getting my baby well. I imagined a long day in hospital then coming home perhaps to put a wash on. I imagined coming back to a peaceful silence, a place where I could recuperate from a long night.

The more I thought about it, the more I realised I would be happier if my house was empty and the rooms silent and mine to cry in if the day was bad, or relax in if it was good. Anyone familiar with Indian customs will know that the usual way of thinking is safety in numbers. Yet, completely against the cultural grain, I craved for isolation. My husband, on the other hand, thought it might be good if someone came for a while. I would have company, maybe we could go out for dinner.

'I don't need any company,' I said. I had to repeat it several times.

The transplant was several months off. Once a donor was found, I would move with my baby to the hospital and live there. The rooms had a bed for parents wanting to stay. The only person allowed in without an apron was the mother because the baby was already habituated to a mother's germs.

Immediately after my parents had exchanged their tickets to an earlier return flight, Dr. Thomas called us. He wanted to see both my husband and me.

He explained the protocol. They would carry out a haplo-identical stem cell transplant – a half matched transplant from one of the parents. After that, we could go home but our baby had to be in complete isolation and stay in the house. We and all our visitors would have to stick rigidly to washing hands every time we came in from outside. We would need to be careful that our visitors weren't unwell themselves. The stem cells, over months, would mature. Every two weeks, we would return to GOSH, for blood tests to check the engraftment of T-cells. There would be immunoglobulin infusions every four weeks.

They would carry out the transplant in the next few days. How fast compared with waiting months for a donor!

'When you have chemotherapy, the B-cells also come back whereas with the half-matched transplant, with no chemo, they don't,' I said, going back to our previous conversation a few days previously. I was trying again to see what he would say.

'Well, we can't generalise in quite such a simplistic way. I would say that with chemotherapy the reconstitution is usually 100% but not always. With a stem cell transplant, there is a full reconstitution in 30% of the cases.'

And then a voice in my head, irrational and loud, said the impossible again. 'His B-cells *will* come back.' It surprised me. The voice was strong and clear. It was midday. My husband and I were sitting opposite Dr. Thomas in one of the consulting rooms, a window on one side, the street outside, nurses busy outside the door on the other side. Yet for a moment, I heard nothing except that voice.

'We can't count on it,' Dr. Thomas was saying. 'We have to assume the B-cells will never come back. See, the reason we don't want to put your baby through chemotherapy is that we have lost young babies to it.' He looked at me directly, as if to gauge my reaction.

'You...you...GOSH has lost babies? I thought you cured everyone with SCID.'

'I wish we could, but chemotherapy can be dangerous and since he is so premature, we don't want to take the risk.'

And neither could we. His words sent a chill through me. Even if we were signing up for a lifetime of monthly infusions of IVIG, or weekly subcutaneous injections of SCIG, there was no other choice. Whatever we were given, we would accept it. We had climbed over enough hurdles and if this was to be our baby's life, we would do our best to help him. My support group mums told many stories, of how their children didn't mind the infusions. How they liked to spend an afternoon off school and get hooked up in the hospital. Or how they spent a couple of hours at the weekend having subcutaneous infusions and got a special treat. I saw pictures of tall, strapping teenagers who were used to their lives with infusions.

Dr. Thomas added his bit. 'I have seen adults who come for their infusions. They hook themselves up. They sit with a book for a couple of hours. It's easy.'

My husband and I looked at each other and knew there was no further discussion, no other options.

'So what are the next steps?' we asked.

'We will take blood samples from both of you and run some tests to check the match. It will take a few days. Once we have the results, we can think about the transplant, maybe by the middle of this month. You could be home by the end of the month if there are no complications, which is what we hope for.'

It was early March. It looked like the end of the tunnel was closer than we had thought.

We told my parents about the change in plan.

'Should we change our tickets again and extend our visit?' they worried.

'I will be fine alone,' I replied.

13

While Dr. Thomas said he would go with the best match, Dr. Radley always used the mother. Her argument was that the mother's cells were always better received by the baby after it had been part of the mother's body for nine months. She usually did the transplant at birth itself, while the mother and baby were in hospital.

Our results showed that my husband was the better match. 8/10. The closer the match, the better the chance of the transplant working. He would have to be the donor.

I had always imagined I would be the donor for my baby. Other mums who had donated for their children had told me all about it. First, I would have G-CSF[17] injections for five days to increase the number of stem cells in the blood. Then, on the day of the transplant, I would be hooked up to a cell separator machine which would pull blood from one arm or leg and return it to the other. The stem cells would be separated from the blood and stored, ready for donation.

Another deciding factor was the presence of viruses such as CMV[18] and EBV[19] which most people would have been exposed to. These lie dormant because most people develop antibodies.

---

17 G-CSF injections: Granulocyte-colony stimulating factor

18 CMV: Cytomegalovirus

19 EBV: Epstein-Barr virus

They aren't a problem for a healthy human being, but for a child with SCID, these viruses, especially CMV, could be dangerous and could reduce the transplant's viability. I knew Dr. Radley never used a CMV positive donor. Our results showed I was CMV negative and EBV positive and my husband tested positive for both CMV and EBV, something that might change the decision about who would be the donor.

I asked Dr. Thomas when he came the next day. I launched into an explanation of how and why I thought I still needed to be considered because CMV could be harmful for a transplant.

'I was wondering how I would get away without answering any questions on CMV,' he said, smiling patiently at me. 'We have learnt to control CMV very effectively. But we may not be able to control a strong case of graft-vs-host disease. That is why I prefer to use the stronger match, rather than a CMV negative donor.'

'Then why doesn't Dr. Radley use CMV positive donors?' My implied question being, *shouldn't you be following the practice of the doctor who invented the method?*

'I am not sure why she doesn't. She must have her reasons. We have used CMV positive donors in the past and not had problems.'

'But Dr. Radley always uses the mother!'

'We normally prefer to use the father as a donor. The machines pulling the blood out are really strong and we can harvest more cells from a larger person. Besides you have just had a caesarean. I don't think we could have used you even if you were a good match.'

It was only four weeks since my surgery. I had still not recovered fully. Yet Dr. Radley would use the mother as the donor straight after the birth. If the other women could go through it, then why not me?

Maybe sensing my disappointment, he said gently, 'It's not an easy process. You have been through enough already. Why are you so keen to be the donor?'

I didn't have a logical answer except that it felt like retribution. I was the person who got him into this situation and I should be the one helping him to get better. I thought as the mother, as the person who bore him, I should be doing more.

He explained again what they were good at, and what they weren't. Sometimes I wondered how he bore my incessant questions with so much patience and amusement. Maybe every mother grilled him or maybe he saw through all my questioning to the worry in my heart and the desire to ensure the best for my infinitely precious baby. The humility and patience of this world-famous doctor was inspirational. My father once commented that if I had posed the same questions to the doctors he worked with in India, they would not have listened to me. The doctors there could sometimes be patronising and condescending, convinced that the patient had little right to question their decisions.

Not once, but repeatedly Dr. Thomas and the other doctors showed how much they cared. Perhaps their concern came from knowing that this was our second baby, conceived with difficulty, and after a hellish time following the tragic loss of our first born. Perhaps they were simply compassionate, professional people whom I was fortunate enough to meet. Either way, I would always see them as the emissaries of grace who were there to help me along.

14

Before leaving, my parents wanted to meet their grandson and cuddle him. They had only seen him through the glass walls of Room 6. The rules were strict. At any one time, there could only be two adults in the room with him. I was usually there, so that meant one other visitor. My mother came in first after washing her hands and putting on the apron. She held him and we took pictures. It was a big day in another sense because we were to try breastfeeding. The doctors said he was strong enough to be taken off the feeding tube and to begin on breast milk. It would be done gradually but even so it was a huge milestone. My mother had wanted to help but by the time she arrived, a nurse had already asked me to try and my baby had latched on from the word go. No reluctance there. My father came in next and was all smiles as he had a brief cuddle. They left the next day – my husband dropping them off at Heathrow – worried yet relieved and full of prayers and wishes that the transplant would go well, that he would be cured and they would come back in a year to spend more time with their precious grandson. We all wanted to spend time together like a normal family.

I now stayed days and nights in GOSH, having no reason to come home.

One afternoon while changing his nappy, I noticed a swelling in his lower abdomen. He had been crying loudly. After a while, the crying stopped and the lump disappeared but I told the doctors.

'Keep a look out and call us if you see it again.'

Sure enough, I saw it again the next day. I pressed the buzzer and the doctor came rushing, first washing her hands and putting on her apron. Not once did a nurse or doctor not wash their hands even if they had washed them a second ago and returned. The nurses showed me their hands at the end of their shifts, chaffed red from the constant washing. They loaded their hands with moisturisers every evening.

'It looks like he has a hernia,' the doctor said. 'It's very common in premature babies.'

A paediatric surgeon was summoned and he fixed a date for an operation that same week. I was frantic.

'Are you sure? What if he gets an infection during surgery? Can't we wait until the transplant has been done? Is it safe? Isn't he too young to go through this?'

I believed it only when Dr. Thomas assured me there was no risk of infection. This wasn't an immunological problem so it wasn't his team carrying out the surgery.

'It is keyhole surgery. He will be fine.'

'But he needs a general anaesthetic. I had one myself. I know.' Of course I know all about it, my manner said.

'Yes he does. But his breathing is stable.'

I had to let go. I had to trust the doctors and nurses. I knew they would remain alert to potential problems.

'When we operate on the left side, we will also check the right and if we find a second hernia, we will do both,' the paediatrician told us.

They found the hernia on one side only. Our baby came back

from the operating theatre sedated and sleeping. While I waited, I had chanted my mantra and prayed.

By evening he was back to his normal self, looking around him, smiling. And the lump was gone.

15

GOSH was home in the middle of London.

'Relax, watch a play, go to the museums,' my husband had encouraged when I had moved in. 'He is in good hands. You can spend the whole day out if you want.'

In fact, I went only once to the British Museum round the corner. My husband visited every evening and then we had dinner in one of the many local restaurants. Some parents ate in the kitchen, some made instant meals. One Asian couple had a large family visiting. They ate together, noisily and cheerfully, in the common area.

Sometimes book stalls were set up downstairs in the main reception area. When I went to get myself my lunch, I would buy myself a book.

At eight every morning, the nurse in charge for the day would come in. From the way the door was opened, I could guess who it was. If it was Madeline, the little eighteen-year-old student nurse, it would be a hasty push and she would be inside in a flash. With barely a look in my direction, she would rush to my baby. She doted on him. When we left, I asked her if she could come and visit us. I dreamed of employing her as a nanny when I eventually got back to work. If the door opened more slowly and there was a cheerful Hi! it would be Rachel, the second-year student aged twenty. She would chat to me as if we were friends.

She too doted on my baby. Then there was Barbara who was a quiet, older nurse, stern until the day she gave my baby his first bath and spiked his hair with water like gel to make him look cool. He wore his *Little but Loud* body suit and smiled. Barbara smiled proudly too and I could see the strong maternal streak beneath her strict exterior.

The transplant nurse, our point of contact, was a beautiful tall girl called Amy. I watched her interact with my baby as if the tubes and machines didn't exist. As if he was the most normal baby she had seen. She changed his nappy and changed his feed, always smiling. One night she took him out of his bed and asked if I wanted him next to me as I fed him.

'Am I allowed to have him on the bed?'

'Of course you are!'

After that night, most nights, he was in my bed and both of us slept soundly until the morning. Those nights meant everything to me.

The morning routine was that the nurse checked him, changed his nappy, checked the feeds and made sure everything was well. I was free and after showering, got some breakfast in the kitchen. By ten, the doctors would arrive and I would watch them through the glass windows of our room. They stood in a huddle to discuss their cases. Then our turn for a visit, sometimes Dr. Rekha, sometimes Dr. Thomas. With him, I always had a lot of questions and I looked forward to seeing him, his smiles, his mild amusement, always positive, always reassuring, just like Mr. Smith.

We were getting closer to transplant day.

My husband was told he would feel unwell while they injected him prior to the transplant so they suggested he should stay somewhere close by that week. The hospital offered free accommodation in flats nearby. Initially reluctant because he could be home by train in thirty minutes, he eventually agreed to stay for two nights. It was good that he did, because the side effects were severe. He spiked a high temperature on the first day. He felt very tired and while the nurses and I teased him that it was typical of a man to complain, I could see he was truly unwell. Those injections were certainly strong and creating quite a stir in his body, forcing the blood cells to multiply, to reproduce in millions so that a large quantity of stem cells could be extracted. I could see now why they preferred to use a man.

16

25th March was the day of the transplant.

In the morning, my husband went to UCL, the sister hospital where the harvest would take place. They hoped to obtain a good volume of stem cells and carry out the transplant by late afternoon or early evening. However, the first harvest could fall short and they would have to repeat the procedure. In that case the harvested stem cells might arrive in Robin Ward too late in the day to continue. We hoped it wouldn't be like that for us.

My husband came back after a couple of hours with the good news that many cells had been harvested. The process had been rough for him. He had been hooked to a giant machine, two tubes were inserted into him, on one side to pull the blood from a vein in the leg and extract the baby-blood cells, and on the other side to return the depleted blood to his body through his arm. Halfway through the extraction process, the vein got blocked so they had to cut through his leg to re-insert the tube. When it was over and he stood up, the dressing gave way and his legs were awash with blood. They asked him if he wanted to rest for a while but thinking he was fine, he left, only to find a fresh flood in the cab. He returned with bloodied jeans to his temporary accommodation.

In the evening the nurse on duty – I was thrilled to see it was Rachel, the young, efficient morning nurse – said the stem cells had arrived. Everyone was ready.

During the stem cell transfusion, my baby could remain in his cot or I could hold him. I said I would hold him on my lap.

'Are you sure? You will need to hold him for a long time.'

'Of course. Yes.'

They expected it to take more than an hour. They helped me get comfortable in the chair and placed a pillow across my lap so that my baby could lie on it. The drip was started into the cannula on his little hand. Stem cells are clear. They dripped through the tube into his body. Drops of life.

He slept peacefully right through it. It was much less scary than a blood transfusion because the stem cells looked innocuous. Dr. Thomas came. He was thrilled that they had harvested a very big dose, as it was called. My husband had reacted strongly to the injections, his body going into overdrive to produce millions of stem cells and that's why he felt so bad. From time to time, they checked my baby's temperature and of course he was still hooked to the machine which checked saturation levels and monitored other functions. Holding him, I said the Maha Mryutunjaya mantra over and over. It was to become a habit over the years. Within a couple of hours, all the magic cells were transplanted from father to son. He literally had his father's blood.

Today was the day I had originally been booked to have a caesarean, the day I would have reached thirty-six weeks. My baby was six weeks old, but technically speaking not even due because he was born eight weeks early. The dates were a strange coincidence. The SCID group called transplant day 'the life day'.

There was nothing to do now but wait. We were instructed to check for any rash, temperature, anything which indicated a possible reaction to the transplant. Since these were stem cells, baby cells and hence less liable to create a reaction, nothing was expected. But they were always cautious. If there was a reaction, it would normally occur within three to five days of the transplant.

A week went by.

He continued to breastfeed until the feeding tube was removed. I couldn't wait. His little fingers could expertly yank the tube out of his nose even when it was taped securely to his little face. And he often pulled it out. Once it was out, of course it had to be put back in and then the cries were deafening. On one occasion, a temporary nurse tried to re-insert the tube in the middle of the night. She couldn't do it and my baby cried louder and louder. I pressed the buzzer which alerted any free medical staff. Within minutes, we were surrounded and one of the senior nurses quickly managed to reinsert the tube.

He only had a couple of soft toys – one pale blue baby bear and a bear rattle – because toys were storehouses for germs. I talked and chatted to him as much as possible. The nurses did the same. He couldn't be taken out of the filtered room so all I could do was take him to the window to look out at the corridors. I wondered what he made of the world he had arrived in.

He had a happy, cheerful vibe about him that everyone commented on and it was only fitting to name him after the playful god Krishna, whose temple I had gone to years ago to pray for a girl child only to find that here you prayed for a son.

A few days later, Dr. Thomas gave us some incredible news. 'He's been stable since the transplant and we haven't seen any adverse reaction. We think you are fine to go home. You will need to come back every week for a check-up and for IVIG infusions every third or fourth week but for now you may as well be at home.'

'Oh, when can we go?'

'We are thinking tomorrow. We need to prepare the discharge papers but that's about it!' He smiled.

Going home! Finally. We had never imagined the day would come so soon. Even though we were not entirely in the clear, it was a huge milestone. But we had no set up at home. We didn't have a car seat, a cot, a bath or supplies. To be home suddenly and responsible for my own meals and all the medication our baby needed was daunting. I had been in various hospitals and under care for almost twenty-four weeks, almost half a year. I was set in my routine. I had made friends with the doctors and nurses. We lived and fought for my baby. These people were my family. The thought of waking up and not having anyone to visit me, not waiting for the doctor to meet me was frightening. Didn't my baby need to be checked and have blood tests every day? What if something went wrong? Would I be able to give him his medication without help from the nurses? I wasn't ready yet!

'Could we just stay a few more days?' I asked.

Dr. Thomas was certainly not expecting that. He almost laughed out loud. Then with a look of infinite patience and amusement, he asked, 'So how long do you want to stay?'

'Maybe we could leave after the Easter break? My husband can go shopping over the long weekend. You see we don't actually have anything for the baby. We never knew what to expect.'

'Of course you can stay until after Easter.' They were all smiling at this unusual request.

We left Great Ormond on the 8th of April, instead of the 4th. Coincidentally, the 8th of April was the day when he would have been full term. It was like leaving home. The older children

277

had a lot of stuff because they recreated their homes in the isolated bubble rooms. But we had only one suitcase, which was mine. Robin Ward and Great Ormond would always be special in my heart. In a way, I couldn't wait for next week when we would come back for our check-up.

Life had indeed brought us challenges, struggles, and surprises. Life had also brought with it an enormous propensity to believe.

I had a stack of medicines. A pack of feeding syringes. Different doses for different times. The nurse on duty had seen to all this. From now on I was everything – the nurse, the doctor, the cook, the mother.

My days, confined indoors to maintain isolation, were one long round of managing his drugs and changing nappies. I watched baby television with him, took umpteen pictures and videos. Bath times were fun because he cried when he was put in and again when taken out. Certainly he was loud. All those fears about his lungs not forming were silenced every time he howled. He was good with his medicines, sucking the syringes. He had prophylactic antiviral medication and penicillin twice a day. The antiviral liquid was bitter beyond belief. I knew because I tasted all his medicines just to see what he had to have. Yet for years he loved the orange penicillin.

The first week at home went quickly. Then it was time to go back to Great Ormond. We went by car because we had to remain in isolation. The congestion charge was reimbursed. Small things to help us with all the big things they had done. Great Ormond was every bit as great I had hoped it would be.

This was a day out for me, meeting the team of nurses and doctors and talking to them about blood tests and how well my baby was feeding. It was like being with caring friends. We had to go back for the IVIG as well and that wasn't so pleasant, but the plan was that eventually that would happen in our local hospital. And a year or two down the line, we could consider the subcutaneous injections, SCIG, but only if the cells didn't come back. I kept my thoughts positive.

Some days later, while changing his nappy, I saw a lump similar to the previous one, on the right side. I hoped I had imagined it, but I called the local surgery. They were up to date since GOSH sent them their reports. Dr. Patel said she would do a home visit and she arrived, beaming and smiling. It was like meeting an old friend who had walked beside me on the journey. She gave me a hug. I proudly showed off the miracle baby and her support and belief made me tearful. If she hadn't been there for us, if Mr. Smith hadn't believed he could help, if Dr. Thomas hadn't thought of following an unusual protocol, if I hadn't met physicians who were confident in their science yet humble enough to believe in something beyond medicine, my story could have been different. I thought of these connections as Divine Grace.

Cutting into my reverie, however, Dr. Patel said my baby did have another hernia. We should contact Great Ormond because we would have to go back there for a further operation. Perhaps the surgeon had missed it, or perhaps the hernia wasn't then sufficiently developed. It was disappointing, but there was nothing for it except do as they advised.

This time we were outpatients so we were in the new building where private patients were admitted. The rooms were large, the staff nice, but it wasn't the same as Robin Ward. I had secretly hoped to be back there but it wasn't to be.

The operation went well and we came home two days later.

We were transferred to the local hospital in Farnborough for IVIG. We were given our own direct access to Admissions so that we didn't have to go through the wards of unwell children. So, straight to the paediatric wards through our special entrance, and we were shown to a single room. They quickly put in a cannula. He cried, but he was too young to know what was happening. Once hooked up to the drip, perhaps he didn't feel anything because he didn't cry. He lay in the cot or on my lap and watched the rattles and other moving toys. Everyone said he was a very happy baby.

I remember once it had been a long day and I had a sandwich with me but nothing to drink. I couldn't get up because I was holding my baby but the nurse found me a Ribena. Not having grown up in the UK, I had never drunk it before. Nor did I ever drink it again but at the time, the cold drink felt like nectar.

My husband had invited his parents to come over for a while. I was literally housebound so if there was someone at home, I could pop out to the shops or the gym and get a break. They came over as summer was arriving and the days were getting longer and warmer.

Around this time, Amy, our transplant nurse, phoned as usual to give me the blood test results. This time, however, proved very special. She told us his T-cells showed signs of reconstitution. This meant the transplant had worked. This meant the stem cells had taken and had matured to functioning T-cells. She said we could now take him out for a walk to open spaces like parks when they weren't too busy.

We went out on a Sunday evening, after the shops were closed and the streets were empty. I pushed the big pram, my husband took pictures in front of the shops, in the small green square.

We walked on the high street, feeling utterly unreal. My baby looked surprised. It was all new to him.

A few weeks later, when the cell count had increased further, we went to Greenwich in the early evening. It was a lovely day and families were having picnics. People were running, playing football, cycling and skateboarding. A vast expanse of sky and grass, trees and people. He stared all around. He was about five months old and while other babies were taking swimming lessons and had been to toddler groups, he was out in a park for the first time in his life. That night he couldn't sleep, possibly from excitement.

We planned many days out after that. We went to Boxhill in Surrey on another bright sunny day. He was around six months and had started on solid food. Instead of preparing fresh food at home, the advice from GOSH was to buy jars of baby food which, though maligned by many, and certainly by most Indians I knew, were actually healthier because they were sterilised and hardly touched by human hands. Krish's preference was clear however. He preferred breast milk to solids. Rejecting solid meals, his little cheeks started to lose their fullness. He was a poor eater and spat out most of the food.

He was also off the prescribed steroids which had to be given after a transplant. They helped suppress the immune system so that there would be no graft-vs-host reaction. Long term use of steroids made cheeks puffy, increased facial hair, and changed a child's appearance. Our child didn't have to be on steroids that long because he hadn't had a full bone marrow transplant.

My in-laws left after a couple of months. By this point, the T cell count was good. We were allowed to go to closed spaces but we were still careful. He was on IVIG, which meant he wouldn't fall ill easily. In fact, children on IVIG were usually healthier than normal children because the infusions provided them with antibodies.

Restaurants dot Russell Square around GOSH. On our day trips for checkups, I would buy a sandwich at Costa or from the canteen. We promised each other that the day he was declared out of isolation, we would have lunch at the Italian at the bottom of the road.

The day came a few months later. The T-cells were 100% reconstituted. Sitting outside, eating a prawn linguine, our baby in the pram, we looked like any other family.

18

When I was in Great Ormond Street Hospital, my manager came to visit and took me out for lunch. I wore my best maternity clothes – a wide pair of navy trousers and a turquoise top – and some make up, and one of the nurses called out, 'You are looking so glamorous!' I hadn't felt glamorous in a long while with my shapeless clothes and I could only laugh.

'You are obviously going through a lot yet you look incredibly calm. How are you really? In yourself?' my boss asked.

Coming from an Englishman, that said a lot about how I appeared to the outside world. I *was* feeling calm. My situation was challenging but I had support and sympathy. When medicine and miracles met, there was no reason to be stressed.

He told me the bully boss was unhappy about leaving my position open which they had to do to comply with maternity laws in the UK. He wondered if I would go back, given my negative experiences and what I had been through now. I didn't want to work for that company but my pragmatic reason for returning was that I was expecting some stock options. I was also planning to look for other jobs. If my search resulted in success, I would happily leave, stock options or not.

'I will come back to work,' I'd told him, as I ate my delicious Italian meal. Even though he seemed to be on my side, I had been burnt enough by the company to not trust anyone. He was surprised but wished me well.

It *was* almost time to think about work. My year of maternity leave was coming to an end. We invited my parents again for a long stay of five months, this time in much more relaxed circumstances. I could attend prospective job interviews once they were here, leaving my baby in their care.

It was also the incredible time of Krish turning one. My parents were overjoyed to be with us to celebrate his first birthday. My husband invited his colleagues and their families for dinner in a Korean restaurant. After all the support they had offered, the unquestioning way they had let my husband have as much time off as he needed, it felt right to celebrate the first birthday with them. Someone proposed to try a Korean custom of the baby choosing an object to predict his career. A pen, stethoscope, a five-pound note were laid out and Krish grabbed the stethoscope with his chubby fingers – a doctor! Everyone was delighted; was it because the stethoscope was so familiar to him? Or was this what he would want to be?

I took him to a toddler group for the first time when he was a year old. I hadn't met any other mothers during my pregnancy or afterwards. I tried to talk to them, all seeming so confident with their friends from birthing groups or other toddler groups and talked about meals, how well their children ate, how they were already walking or talking at nine months and how well they did at swimming lessons. Each told stories full of pride. I looked at my baby and thought about what he had been through. He didn't even know that other babies existed let alone how much they could do. The house and hospital were his homes, his bubble. Yet he looked the brightest and happiest baby as he crawled around. Or maybe that was just me.

The immunoglobulin infusions now took place at home with a nurse coming in from the local hospital. They hoped soon I would learn to administer SCIG at home. I would have to insert a needle in each thigh, under the skin, and the infusion lasted between thirty and sixty minutes. I had injected myself with Clexane for months during my pregnancy, so I assumed I knew all about jags and could do this. But as he grew older, Krish was becoming more aware of what was happening to him – the cream to numb his skin, the needles, the staying still for a couple of hours. No longer a baby who would stay still and sleepy in my lap, he wanted to crawl away and grab things. And he was beginning to understand pain. My friends in the SCID group told me it got easier once children were old enough to understand how vital it all was but before that, it would get more difficult. Try explaining to an active toddler that they need infusions every four weeks or subcutaneous injections every two weeks.

I was in tears watching him cry, trying to hold him still while the nurse found the right spot to push the needle in. My father fidgeted then went upstairs, then came down again. My mother remained upstairs, away from the din.

'I don't like it. I don't want to accept this,' she said when it was over for this time. Only to be done again in another few weeks.

'Your liking or not liking it makes no difference,' I said. 'He has to go through this all his life. The whole of his life! Don't you get it? It is up to me to make this a part of his normal routine. He's got to accept it.'

'His B-cells will come back,' she said stubbornly. 'He won't need this always.'

A diya[20] burned brightly on the window sill, the flame unwavering. It was yet another offering to one of the many gods my mother prayed to. 'Every time he has an infusion, I will light the diya and ensure it burns for the duration.'

'Well, if that brings the B-cells back, do it, but we know the chances are slight. We have to accept that and cope.'

I sounded practical but I was distraught. How could he go through so much every month? And even if he got used to it, as people said he would, could I get used to it? I imagined taking a day off work every month to sit through tears and infusions. Of explaining to a young boy how vital they were to maintain his quality of life. Without them, he would always have to be a boy in a bubble.

There were two other boys in the support group who had a 100% functioning immune system after being treated by Dr. Radley. Irrational wishes and dreams rose again. Why couldn't my baby be the third? Hadn't the voice told me his B-cells would come back when Dr. Thomas was explaining the process?

---

20 Diya: like a tea-light candle, except it is earthen and uses oil to burn. Used in festivals such as Diwali and for worshipping in temples

19

And then incredibly, one day, around a year after the transplant, Amy told us that the blood test results suggested there were traces of B-cells. She also warned us it may mean nothing. Sometimes B-cells showed up but they were useless and non-functioning.

'So how do you know if they are working?'

'The only way we know is to stop infusions for several months, then vaccinate him and then see how he responds to the vaccine.'

When a child is on IVIG infusions, there is no need to be vaccinated. In fact, if the B-cells, which help create antibodies, don't work, then it's pointless giving vaccinations. When you are on IVIG, you stay healthy because IVIG is an infusion of B-cells from many, many donors and you receive the mass immunity developed by them.

'We will see how it goes, and if the trend is an increase in his B-cell counts, we will consider taking him off the infusions as a trial to check if they work.'

But they would work. They had to, I told myself, as if my mind could force those B-cells into action.

Initially our visits to GOSH were weekly, then every two weeks, and now once a month. Sometimes we met Dr. Thomas but usually one of the other doctors. While they were all good, I felt more reassured with Dr. Thomas and always had several questions for him.

'What if he becomes unwell when we stop the IVIG?' I asked him at our next appointment.

'His T-cells show good reconstitution. If he catches something, we are confident the T-cells will work and fight the infection. We're not worried about an experimental stopping of the IVIG.'

'Do we need to be back in isolation when he is taken off IVIG?' My parents were here and we had planned some short trips to Europe. Could we travel if he wasn't on immunoglobulins?

'No, you don't need to be in isolation. Live normally. You can go out anywhere, closed spaces, on flights. It's best that he leads a normal life.'

By now, I trusted him completely. If he said something wasn't a risk, it wasn't one. I did not quiz him anymore.

When the B cell count rose the following month as well, they decided to take him off IVIG for three months in the summer, the best time to try it. He would be vaccinated with DPT which babies are given at birth and if he showed a healthy reaction, he would be given all the childhood vaccines. The one he could never be given was BCG, the one that had taken such a severe toll on my first baby. BCG is a live vaccine and is never given to an immuno-compromised child.

We applied for a passport. The date of issue was 22nd October. The birthday of his brother.

We went to Bruges and Brussels. We went to Rome. Krish was a happy traveller, thrilled to be on flights, never upset when the plane took off and landed. Like typical tourists, we walked the cities, pushing him along in his big pram. After the stress of the last trip, my parents were delighted and relaxed.

Three months passed without immunoglobulins.

He received his first DPT vaccine. We waited for the results with bated breath.

I prayed. I prayed all the time, even when I played with my baby, when I watched him sleep, and I hoped that the result would be the one I wanted to hear. When I rang to ask, it was Amy who answered. 'He has mounted a response to the DPT vaccine. And his...'

'Sorry what does that mean? Does that mean he responded to the vaccine?' I interrupted rudely.

'Yes! Absolutely. We are delighted. This means his B-cells are working!'

The miracle was slow, ever so slow, but it was happening.

Soon after the DPT, he was given other routine vaccinations and his reactions were monitored. For some there was a satisfactory response but not all. Dr. Thomas explained that there were pockets or gaps in his immune system which would always remain. It didn't mean we needed to restrict his lifestyle but we would always need to be vigilant about hygiene including hand washing, and being extra careful when travelling outside Europe. India would always be a challenge, and in the years to come, preparations to visit India would be very stressful for me. I would always worry about mosquitoes and flies as well as all the diseases prevalent in a tropical country. People assumed I was behaving like a first world returned snob. And even relatives who did know our past could never quite grasp why a single mosquito would give me such extreme anxiety and why my son, always smelling of mosquito repellent, wore long sleeved t-shirts in a hot country.

I thought back to the quadrant I had drawn, and knew I had been wrong. The miracle was the result in the top left quadrant, not the right. The real miracle was after you worked to your bones, when you believed with the core of your soul, and the result was sweeter than anything you could have hoped for.

Watching him smile made me believe in the power of prayer, in grace, in the impossible becoming reality.

My maternity leave had ended and I hadn't found another job. Employers didn't seem convinced by a new mother interviewing whilst on maternity leave. While in India, women went back to work with very young babies, as I had myself, but in the UK it wasn't usual. Most women went on to have more babies so companies didn't want to take the risk of employing them. I had a greater chance of finding a new job while I was working so I returned to my old job with reluctance, yet brushed with a new confidence. I found I could look the bully boss in the face and say, 'I need to leave now,' when he asked the team to meet him at six in the evening in a hotel lounge for a catch up. I calmly said goodbye and left. He looked shocked.

I worked mostly from home and went to meetings once or twice a week. The ideal job would be higher paid and allow me to work from home all the time or for a significant part of the week with only occasional travel overseas. I wrote down my wish and tried to visualise it strongly. It was a tall order, in fact almost impossible.

Day care was not an option for us because small children carried and passed so many germs to one another. Although Krish didn't need to be in isolation, constant exposure to germs wasn't recommended. I wrote to an agency and read a string of résumés. It was a daunting task. I blamed my parents because they had spoiled him when I was at work so now no one else would be able to manage him. It didn't help that he was a real mummy's boy and clung to me like a koala bear.

We interviewed three nannies and the one we liked didn't like us. Time was short with my parents' stay coming to an end. We finally made an offer to a woman with twenty years experience. She spent most of the day sitting on the sofa like a guest, watching us as we went about our chores. We worried that we seemed a mad chaotic household in this quiet woman's eyes.

We walked to a toddler group nearby. Because she didn't say a word to Krish, I told her she needed to interact with him more by pointing out buses and cars and birds and engaging his attention. He was a bright child and interested in his surroundings. Later, the other mums suggested she was three times my size, so I needed to find someone more like me because babies take to people who remind them of their own mother. They commented on how passive she was. 'She doesn't seem to respond to anything. How will she react in an emergency?'

Finally, my mother said it was stressing her to have a woman sitting on the sofa all day doing nothing, staring at them and the baby. We had to find someone else. It was hard to admit that we had made a mistake and she wasn't the right choice.

Meanwhile I made it through the first round of an interview for a job with a company that was perfect: the salary, the working from home, only occasional travelling, the team. It ticked every single box on my check list.

And I was back to interviewing nannies. I told them all about SCID and the transplant because they needed to understand the important role they would play in our lives and that we needed to trust them to be alert to problems.

A new string of nannies arrived for interview – some very young, some very confident, and all very set in their ways.

Not one seemed interested in Krish as he crawled around on the floor. They just tried to impress me. After every interview I asked myself how I could think of leaving my precious baby with someone else? Should I be thinking of going back to work?

My father had picked one résumé as his favourite. 'Something about this girl makes me think she will be the one,' he had said, looking at her photo. She was the last one on our list.

She came in, a young, sweet faced girl, sat on the sofa and answered my questions politely like all the others until Krish crawled in. Immediately, she was on the floor. I was busy describing her duties but she was engrossed, talking to him. Wonder of wonders, for the first time he was interested in someone other than me. He grabbed her bracelet. He smiled at her. The girl kept talking to him. My father had to take him out of the room so we could complete the interview in peace and she would listen to me instead. When they came back in from the garden, Krish held some violets in his chubby fingers. My father suggested he give them to the girl and he held out the flowers. When she left, she took the crushed flowers with her. We looked at each other in disbelief.

I made her an offer but still cautious, asked her to come just for a few hours to start with. She wanted to take him to the park for a while. I tried to put him in the pram. He protested, like he always did when I put on his harness. He hated any kind of restraint. I was used to his protests so I carried on. She fell to her knees on the floor and started singing in a clear voice, *'Krish, Krish it's a lovely day. Krish, Krish we are going out to play. Krish, put your hat on, tell your mummy you won't be long....'* Incredible! Krish gurgled. She tied the pram belt, singing all the while and he, smiling, let her. Tears filled my eyes. They went out in the sun.

A couple of weeks later, I was offered the job I wanted.

And just like that, everything fell into place. Life stitched itself back into a million colours.

SECTION 6 – REFLECTIONS – FAITH

I have learnt that if you let go and live with a prayer in your heart, you will be held strong. If you fall, you will fall holding that prayer and that in itself will lift you back up.

I have learnt that if you really want something, want something so badly that you can't imagine living without it, it will happen and you will treasure what you have been given all the more because you hoped so hard. You have to accept the gift wholeheartedly and with gratitude.

I have learnt that words are powerful and can protect you. I have learnt that miracles happen and that love and prayer can take you far.

I know that you have to hold closely to your beliefs but even in moments of darkness, your faith will see you through the struggles and challenges.

I know that even when you feel that life is unfair, the story you live is your very own. Your story must continue and you will learn from it.

I have learnt that if you can move beyond trivial worries, you can find something miraculous. The path to a miracle may be stony and hard, but the destination is worthwhile.

I know that the future may not be perfect. I know there may be challenges ahead. There may be pain. There may be heartbreak. I cannot see the future nor can I control it so I will live in the moment. This moment is all I have in which to give my very best, now and always.

It is all out there. Inspiration and glory, faith and the power of prayer, wishes and dreams, even miracles. That is what I hold on to.

ACKNOWLEDGMENTS

This book took its first breath one evening when the life writing piece I'd submitted as part of coursework for my Masters in Creative Writing was being workshopped. Professor Carolyn Hart and classmates including Molly Rikvin, James Napier, Tom Walton, Dean Music and Alan Devy gently, then firmly, suggested I should write it as a full length memoir. Thank you all, especially Alan Devy, for reading and editing a very early draft and Carolyn Hart for your constant encouragement and faith in my writing. Without that initial push from you all, I wonder if I would ever have plunged into writing this book.

Thank you Claire Gilman and Writers' Workshop for the positive manuscript evaluation report and useful comments. Jamilah Ahmed for that email which helped more than you will ever guess. Jennifer Berger-Gross, our shared stories, thanks for your proffered help when the book was still forming. Neel Mukherjee for very kind email and help.

Thank you SCID group, my lifeline for years, you and your families are my strength. Aditi Chaudhary, Heather Smith, Barb Ballard, Evelyn Chiasson, Allison Sparrowhawk, Karen Robertson-Browne, Lynette Westfall, Allison Fillery, Lisa Waugh, Julie Schwarz, Deni Berger, Dawn Strickler, Michelle Worley, and everyone else for the information, love, support. Thank you for being so brave.

Thank you PPROM support group, so many emails exchanged sharing our days. Thank you Netmums message board, especially Michelle Barber, for years of emails and love.

And my friends who were there for me at some point on my journey, for your small or big gestures: a call, a visit, fund-raising, reading early versions of the manuscript. Perhaps you don't even remember what you did but I always will. Sanghamitra Rath, Madhumita Mohanty, Susmita Misra, Sabyasachi Dasmohapatra, Binod Panda, A Ravindra, Sambit Mohapatra, K.K. Menon, Koushik Chatterjee, Arnab Das, Sharmi Roy, my colleagues in Ushacomm Calcutta and Ushacomm UK (2000), Jagdish Mahapatra, Mahesh Rao, Seema Ravani, Prashant Jajodia, Swagata Basu, Banoja Acharya, Alexia Hanson, Pragyan Paramita, Katie-Ann Woolcott and the Woolcott family, Lulu Leach, Melvyn Burgoyne, Rajesh Chandiramani, Laura Mittal, Ambika Mahapatra, Subhendu Mohanty, Mr. Lim, Dr. Koo, Mr. Jeon and the Samsung Investments team.

And my loving family especially A.S. Kumar, Dr. Leena Appicatla, Aniketh Mohanty, Shraddha Appicatla, Subhakanta Nanda, T.K. Misra, Maya Misra, Ashok Misra, Rajashri Mahapatra, Dr. K.C Misra, Mrs. Bimalprabha Rath, Kaumudi Mishra, Sushant Mishra, Kausik Misra and Mamta Mishra for yout help and visits.

And very specially, beloved parents, Mamata Dash and Dr. R.N. Dash. Nothing would have been possible without you.

The wonderful doctors I was so fortunate to meet, Dr. Cherian, Dr. Paranjape, Dr. Pushparajah, Professor Gaspar, Mr. Steer, Nurse Lucy and Nurse Jinhua, thank you.

The staff and nurses at Chelsfield Hospital, Farnborough Hospital, Queen Charlotte Hospital, Guy's and St.Thomas',

King's College, Great Ormond Street Hospital. I don't know all your names but your support and kindness will always stay with me.

The Whole Kahani for leading me to Linen Press.

The Linen Press team: Alison Donn, Eve Kerr and Sophie Burdge.

And finally Lynn Michell, publisher, editor, dynamo woman with a heart, for adopting this manuscript from the time you read it and took it up with love, through to the patient and fierce editing. We have had many moments together working late in the night, early in the morning, on trains and planes, including hilarious incidents of disappearing footnotes, and exploding eggs when I was so absorbed in your comments I forgot all about my boiling breakfast egg. Your emails always engrossed me and I will miss them. Thank you for walking beside me as I went on my journey all over again. Thank you for holding my hand, word after word.